Debts, Defaults, Depression and Other Delightful Ditties from the Dismal Science

Dr. Bryan Taylor
Chief Economist
Global Financial Data

Published by

Global Financial Data
29122 Rancho Viejo Rd. Suite 215
San Juan Capistrano, CA 92675

Contents

Illustrations

Tables

Acknowledgments

I would like to thank Michelle Kangas for her invaluable help in reviewing and editing the chapters in this book. She has provided useful insights into making each chapter more interesting and appealing to the average reader. Her focus on what part of each chapter to emphasize and expand, which portions to remove, how to make each chapter funny and interesting, and providing intriguing taglines for many of the sections helped to ensure the book is fun to read and not a soporific study in economics.

I would like to thank my editors, Erica Orloff and Jon VanZile for all their suggestions for improving the book. I also received insights and valuable feedback from Maureen Burton, Mike Cerneant, Josh Silverman and Pierre Gendreau and would like to thank them for their suggestions.

part one

Golden Dreams

chapter one

Is Gold a Good Long-Term Investment?

In August 1999, gold traded at $252.50 an ounce. After that, the price of gold rose to $1,900 an ounce in September 2011 before declining to the $1,200 range in the beginning of 2017. Despite these ups and downs, many people feel that gold could rise above $2,000 within a few years. Gold is seen as a safe haven against inflation and economic uncertainty, and can rise in price when the value of other financial assets decline.

Is gold a good long-term investment? Although this chapter isn't designed to provide advice on investing in gold, it does provide investors with a long-term perspective on the performance of gold relative to other asset classes and other commodities.

The Gold Standard

Gold is a special commodity because for centuries it was the metal upon which the global economy stood. In 1914, most European countries and the United States were on the gold standard, which meant that gold was a legal tender for payments within each country, and gold was used to settle international payments; however, not all countries were on the gold standard. Many developing countries were on a gold exchange standard, which meant that they pegged their paper currencies to currencies that were convertible into gold. Other countries were on a silver standard, rather than a gold standard, making silver a legal tender within the country. Since the supply of silver increased faster than the supply of gold in the 1800s, a silver standard was more inflationary than a gold standard.

Advocates who support a return to a gold standard argue that the gold standard would control inflation by limiting the ability of the central banks to increase the money supply to cover government deficits.

Before 1914 when gold was the basis of the international economy, and central banks were unable to print as much money as they wanted, inflation was minimal. Since the gold standard has been abandoned, inflation has been higher than at any other time in history because many countries lack the independence needed to control growth in the money supply.

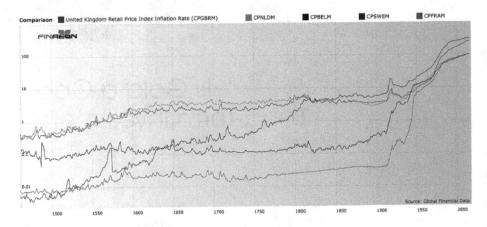

Figure 1.1 Consumer Prices for the United Kingdom, the Netherlands, Belgium, Sweden and France from 1462 to 2010.

Figure 1.1 shows the path of consumer prices in five European countries from 1462 to 2010, a period of over 500 years. In four (Great Britain, the Netherlands, Belgium and France) of the five countries, there was virtually no inflation between 1615 and 1915. The exception to this rule was Sweden, which was the first country to have a central bank. Sweden relied on copper plates as a form of money during the 1600s and 1700s because of Sweden's relative poverty. These copper plates weighed 10 to 20 pounds and were too heavy for most people to carry around. But don't worry, the rich had muscle-bound servants to carry their money around for them.

The Sveriges Riksbank was founded in 1668 and issued paper currency which was easier to carry then copper plates. Not surprisingly, the first country with a central bank also suffered the most inflation during the era of the gold standard.

Over the past 100 years, however, countries have relied upon central banks for their monetary policy, and as can be seen in Figure 1.1, each country has suffered more inflation in the last 100 years than in the previous 500 years put together. It is because of the desire to end the inflation, that some people favor a return to a gold standard.

Although inflation has been relatively mild so far in the twenty-first century, there is still a fear that central banks will keep pushing for an expansion in the money supply causing higher inflation, and that at some point, central banks could lose control, and inflation will return.

Should the United States Return to a Gold Standard?

In order to return to a gold standard, the government would have to set the price of its currency equal to a set amount of gold and be willing to sell gold at that rate to any individual or any government. In the United States, the price of gold was fixed at $20.67 between 1873 and 1933 and $35 from 1933 to 1973. Since then, the United States has been off of the gold standard.

Some advocates of the gold standard argue that if the United States returned to the gold standard, the government would need to set the price of gold in the range of $2,000. Only at that price, could the government guarantee converting all dollars it has issued into gold. Consequently, they conclude that gold is undervalued and will rise in price in the future.

But this raises the question, why did the United States and other countries leave the gold standard to begin with? The answer is simple: World War I.

Before 1914, the government represented a small portion of gross domestic product (GDP), and the only times when government expenditures represented a large share of GDP was during a war or a revolution when the government was unable to raise sufficient taxes to meet its needs. Britain went off the gold standard during the Napoleonic Wars, the U. S. during the Civil War, France during the French Revolution, and every country during World War I.

Although some people have visions of using gold coins to pay for their groceries, if the United States returned to the gold standard, using gold for everyday transactions would be highly unlikely. In 1914, when the United States left the gold standard, per capita income in the United States was about $400, so a $20-gold piece represented about two to three weeks' salary for the average person, or about $2,500 using today's average per capita income. Although individuals would have the right to convert payments into gold, even if the United States returned to a gold standard, individuals would still rely largely on electronic payment for most transactions.

Advocates of a new gold standard argue that it would impose fiscal discipline on governments, forcing them to control spending and deficits. In reality, this is highly unlikely. In the 1800s, the government represented 5 to 10 percent of GDP, but today, the government represents around 40 percent of GDP in the United States. During the 2008 to 2009 recession, the U.S. government deficit exceeded 10 percent of GDP, more than total federal expenditures during most of the nineteenth century.

Although a gold standard imposes discipline, it also limits the flexibility the government has to respond to a crisis. In reality, even when the gold standard existed and the government's role in the economy was small, governments suspended the gold standard and switched to fiat money, i.e. paper money that had no intrinsic value and was money because the government said it was money, whenever it was necessary because of war or some other emergency.

One of the primary purposes of the gold standard was to provide an international medium of exchange through which international imbalances could be settled, but if only a few countries were on the gold standard, the role of gold in the international economy would be minimal or non-existent. A new gold standard would be unlikely to succeed unless a new Bretton Woods Agreement established the gold standard throughout the world.

The real question is whether fiscal discipline creates the conditions for the gold standard to succeed, or whether the gold standard in and of itself can impose fiscal discipline. Advocates of the gold standard believe it would control government spending because the government would no longer have fiat money to support its deficits. However, those who advocate returning to the gold standard are probably putting the cart before the horse.

History shows that the gold standard has almost always been sacrificed to the needs of the government, rather than the other way around. The goal of returning to a gold standard is to eliminate the inflationary bias of fiat money, but if the government were able to exercise fiscal discipline to begin with, returning to the gold standard would be a moot point. Countries such as Germany and Switzerland, which have exercised greater fiscal discipline than the United States since World War II, have seen their currencies rise in value against the U.S. dollar. In 1950, a U.S. dollar commanded 4.3 Swiss Francs. In 2017, a Swiss Franc was worth about 1 U.S. dollar.

For all these reasons, it seems unlikely that the world would or could return to a gold standard in the twenty-first century with the price of gold pegged to $2,000 per ounce. Even if there were a return to the gold standard, governments would leave the gold standard whenever they found it necessary. If we assume a return to the gold standard is unlikely, then how well has gold done as an investment over the past 100 years?

Has Gold Been a Good Long-Term Investment?

Gold increased in price fivefold between August 1999 and February 2017. But is the current rise in the price of gold a short-term, cyclical or a long-term secular move? How has gold performed relative to other asset classes?

Over the past 100 years, equities (represented by the S&P 500 Total Return Index) have provided the highest return to investors of any asset class. Government bonds have provided the next best returns, and the three other asset classes, treasury bills, gold and oil have all barely beaten inflation. In short, gold has been a poor investment relative to its alternatives during the past 100 years.

There are several important facts that can be of benefit to investors. First, gold is countercyclical to equities. Gold rose in price both during the 1970s and in the 2000s when the stock market stalled, but underperformed when equities did well in the 1940s, 1950s, 1980s and 1990s.

Second, gold is often seen as a hedge against inflation, but over the long term, gold barely beat inflation. In 1999 when the current bull market in gold began, the price of gold was lower, after adjusting for inflation, than it had been in 1910.

Third, gold may enjoy periodic bull markets, but there is a reversion to the mean after each bull market ends. The U.S. government raised the price of gold from $20 to $35 in 1933, but kept the nominal price at that level for the next 40 years, thus causing a real depreciation in the price of gold. The bull market in gold during the 1970s was followed by a 20-year bear market in the 1980s and 1990s. Between 2011 and 2015, the price of gold declined as interest rates fell close to zero, and the government got its fiscal house in order.

How has gold performed relative to other commodities? Other metals have performed about the same as gold. Over the long term, most metals are able to keep up with inflation, but they do not beat inflation. If this behavior persisted over the past 100 years, there is little reason to believe it will be any different in the next hundred years. Metals do show periodic bull markets which investors can exploit, and metals experienced a bull market between 2009 and 2012; however, bull markets in commodities occur primarily when other asset markets are in disarray. Once growth and stability return to the economy, commodities fall into long-term bear markets in which they underperform relative to other asset classes.

Is Gold a Good Long-Term Investment?

To answer our original question, the answer is no if you are looking at a period of 10 or 20 years. Gold and other metals underperform both stocks and bonds in the long run. Commodity prices may keep up with inflation, but they rarely beat inflation.

chapter two

Which Came First, the Goose or the Golden Egg? Returning to the Gold Standard in Five Easy Steps

You hear some people in the United States talking about returning to the gold standard. This was especially true after the 2008 financial crisis when the government ran a half a trillion-dollar annual deficit, and economic uncertainty was high. Some people felt a return to the gold standard would help stabilize the economy and force the government to be more financially and fiscally conservative. Currently, the United States issues a fiat currency, which has no backing and whose intrinsic value depends upon the government's credibility.

Some people feel the Fed has done a poor job of maintaining the value of the U.S. dollar since its establishment in 1914, and that a fiat currency gives the federal government too much freedom to spend money since it can print more dollars and issue more debt to cover any federal government deficits. Returning to the gold standard would be one way of controlling government spending. The gold standard could also provide price stability because it would eliminate the "freedom" provided by a fiat currency to print more money at will and impose fiscal responsibilities on the government that are often ignored.

What is rarely heard in this debate is if the United States actually decided to return to the gold standard, how would it get there? What steps would have to be taken in order to return the United States to a fully functioning gold standard similar to the one that existed throughout the world prior to World War I? Here is how it could be done in five easy steps.

Step 1: Declare the Value of the U.S. Dollar in Terms of Gold

The United States issued gold coins during most years between 1795 and 1933 when the United States abandoned the gold standard and made it illegal (until

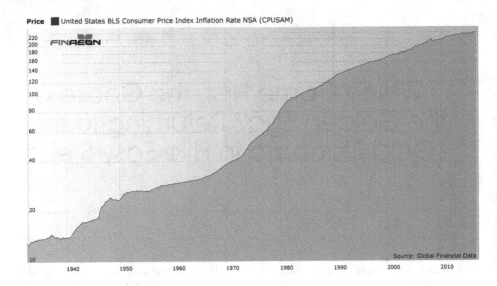

Figure 2.1 United States Consumer Price Index, 1933 to 2015.

1974) for Americans to own gold. Under the gold standard, the value of the U.S. dollar was set at $20.67. A $20 gold piece contained almost 1 ounce of gold and existed as a medium of exchange.

Given the inflation that has occurred in the United States since 1933 (Figure 2.1), it would be unrealistic to return to the old price of gold at $20.67, especially since the price was raised to $35 under Roosevelt and $42.22 under Nixon before the government abandoned gold completely.

One simple solution would be to devalue federal reserve notes and declare that 100 federal reserve dollars are equal to 1 gold dollar. This would set the value of gold in terms of the U.S. dollar at $2,067. Since this rate is higher than the market price, the government's announcement would attract gold into the U.S. Treasury so the United States could replenish its gold reserves. Of course, this action would lead to some inflation in the United States and possible depreciation of the U.S. dollar, but that would be one cost of moving to a gold standard.

Once the value of the U.S. dollar was redefined at $2,067 an ounce, the United States would have to maintain that price. As long as the market price of gold was at $2,067 or below, the U.S. government would buy any gold it was offered. But what would happen if the market price exceeded $2,067?

If the market price of gold were to exceed the predefined $2,067, people would simply stop selling gold to the U.S. Treasury at that price. In the old days, this would cause an outflow of gold to other countries offering a higher relative price for gold, but until other countries joined the gold standard (The euro might be set at 1,800 euros = 1 ounce of gold or 1,500 British pounds = 1 ounce of gold, etc.), there would be no foreign government treasury the gold could flow into.

Instead, the gold would flow into private hands. The United States would have to take measures to push the market price of gold back to $2,067 to defend the gold dollar. The government could do this by either raising interest rates, increasing the return on gold dollars, or by introducing monetary policies that would cause deflation. In the short run, financial flows determine the value of currencies, so the focus would be on using monetary policy to maintain the fixed price of gold. This would lead to step 2.

Step 2: Change the Federal Reserve's Mission to Maintaining the Value of the Gold Dollar

Currently, the Federal Reserve has several goals it tries to achieve. The Federal Reserve is supposed to simultaneously control inflation, keep unemployment at acceptable levels, promote growth and employment in the economy, maintain the value of the U.S. dollar and promote a stable financial system. The problem is some of these goals run contrary to each other. Reducing unemployment may contribute to inflation, while controlling inflation may slow growth and increase unemployment. So the Fed has to determine which of these goals is the most important at any point in time, and focus on that goal at the expense of the others. If the economy is in a recession, the Fed decides to promote growth even if some inflation occurs. If inflation is spiraling out of control, the Fed fights inflation even though it may slow growth and lead to some unemployment.

The benefit of returning to a gold standard is that it simplifies life for the Fed tremendously. No more worrying about unemployment and growth, just focus on maintaining the value of the U.S. dollar relative to gold. During the 1800s, there were long periods of deflation and slow growth that occurred and this could become a possibility after the gold standard was reintroduced. On the other hand, under a gold standard there would be little need to worry about double-digit inflation slowly destroying the value of assets and the U.S. dollar.

Returning to a gold standard would also mean an end to financial bubbles since there is no expansion of fiat currency to keep the bubble going. A gold standard means stable asset prices as well as stable prices for goods. As in the 1800s, stock market prices might change little from one decade to the next because stock prices would respond to real, not inflated profits. Homeowners wouldn't have to worry about housing prices rising and making housing unaffordable (but existing homeowners couldn't expect the value of their houses to rise every year either). A return to the gold standard would mean that money that would have been channeled into assets for speculation could be redirected to real assets.

Of course, someone might ask, if the gold standard worked so well in the 1800s, why did countries abandon it? Simple, almost every time a country left the gold standard it was caused by one thing: government deficits. During the 1800s, most governments were relatively small, so government deficits were almost always caused by war. Great Britain suspended the convertibility of paper pounds into gold during the Napoleonic Wars, and the United States (both the Union and the Confederacy) suspended the convertibility of paper dollars during the Civil War. However, in both these cases, after the wars were over, the countries deflated, governments maintained budget surpluses, and governments paid down existing debt to return to the gold standard.

What really killed the gold standard more than anything else was World War I. The levels of debt, the economic dislocations and the post-war costs associated with the Great War were so huge that returning to the old fixed rates of gold proved impossible. Britain's attempt to return to the pre-war definition of gold devastated the economy. Although there were numerous international conferences during the 1920s and 1930s that attempted to reinstitute the gold standard, these attempts all failed. With no international agreement, each country chose to use fiscal and monetary expansion to spur their economies to recover.

But if the United States moved back to the gold standard, it would have to return to fiscal stability so there would be no threat of the United States being forced to suspend the convertibility of paper dollars into gold dollars. Hence, step 3.

Step 3: Pass a Balanced Budget Amendment to the United States Constitution

Of course, Congress would not only have to pass a Balanced Budget Amendment, but give the amendment credibility so that other countries as well as America's own citizens knew that balancing the budget was paramount over all other fiscal goals. In an age when the U.S. Congress can't even pass a budget and uses continuing resolutions as a way of keeping the government from grinding to a halt, this would be a huge step.

To give full credibility to this goal, the United States would need to add a Balanced Budget Amendment to the U.S. Constitution. This would require the bill's passage by two-thirds of both houses of Congress and then ratification by three-fourths of the states. Some would argue that this would take a long time, but that isn't necessarily so. When the United States decided to end Prohibition, Congress proposed the Twenty-First Amendment on February 20, 1933, and it was adopted through state-ratifying conventions on December 5, 1933. And let's be honest here, isn't balancing the budget more important than getting drunk? It's just a matter of setting priorities.

Of course, it isn't necessary to pass a balanced budget every single year in order to maintain the new gold standard, or to pay off existing federal government debt. Britain spent a century gradually paying down the costs of the Napoleonic wars. The key is that the government should provide credibility to maintaining the fixed price of one ounce of gold at $2,067 U.S. dollars.

So what could go wrong?

1. **War.** This is what usually pushed countries off the gold standard. Countries were simply unable to raise taxes enough to pay for a war, so they borrowed money and paid off the debt over time. This means that if the United States wants to fight a war abroad, wars mean higher taxes under a gold standard, not adding to the deficit.

2. **Social Security.** When the gold standard existed in the 1800s, there was no Social Security. One of the principal fears that people have concerning future budgets is the impact of rising Social Security costs on budget deficits. Adopting the gold standard does not mean abandoning Social Security, but to stay on the gold standard, the United States would have to provide credibility to limiting expenditures on Social Security. The easiest way would be to allocate a fixed amount of GDP to Social Security expenditures each year and never breech that amount. The retirement age could be raised, and/or means testing could be introduced to reduce future Social Security costs. Each year, Social Security benefits would have to adjust to fit within those limits. This might mean lowering Social Security benefits in some years if the economy shrank or was in a recession, or a form of the negative income tax could be used as a kind of means testing. Either way, Social Security would have to take second place to maintaining the gold standard.

3. **Medicare and Medicaid.** Compared to the projected growth in the costs of Medicare as the Baby Boomers age and medical technology advances and costs increase, Social Security is a minor concern. The only way to control medical expenditures is to provide less medical care. In order to maintain balanced budgets, the government would have to cap medical spending. This could be done in several ways. Co-pays could be expanded, payments could be tied to the health of the individual, and caps could be placed on total government expenditures on each person. Some estimates have shown that current Medicare recipients receive three times as much in benefits as they paid in. Obviously, this is unsustainable. Like any insurance program, expenditures and revenues must balance. Inevitably, restricting health care expenditures would mean denying some medical care and making a cost-benefit analysis of medical care a priority over trying to extend life no matter what the cost. If the government never says no, medical costs will never stop rising.

4. **Other Government Transfers.** The federal government transfers large amounts of money to the states, municipalities and foreign governments, and provides bailouts to banks and corporations. Under a gold standard, no private or public entity should be allowed to receive transfers from the federal government. If states issue bonds to spend money they don't have and they can't pay those bonds, they default. If businesses fail, they go bankrupt. If banks fail, they shut their doors. If governments default, creditors have to bear the costs. The federal government could, in some cases, act as a lender of last resort when liquidity is a problem, but bailouts for insolvency that imperil the balanced budget would have to end.

5. **Countercyclical Fiscal Policy.** Followers of English economist John Maynard Keynes encourage the government to run deficits during recessions and surpluses during expansions to pay off the accumulated debts. The problem is that governments are good at running deficits during recessions, but poor at running

surpluses during expansions to pay off the incurred debt. Any current deficit would have to be fully offset by future surpluses. Without a guarantee of a future surplus, the deficit could not be incurred. Hoping fiscal policy will balance itself of its own accord would have to be abandoned. After all, if I never had to pay off my credit cards, I would run deficits every month as well.

Assuming that none of the consequences of restricting fiscal policy to maintain a balanced budget and adhere to the new gold standard is unacceptable, what would be the next step?

Step 4. Elect Gold-Standard Politicians

Given the current (or maybe eternal is a better word) low standing of politicians, this might be the most difficult step of all. And if the government virtually collapses over raising the debt ceiling, what would happen if it debated introducing a new gold standard?

If politicians want to redeem themselves, this could be one way of doing so. It shouldn't be forgotten that during the period from 1795 to 1933 when the United States issued gold coins, there were constant political battles over the gold standard and its consequences. Whether it was how the new United States dealt with the debts incurred by the Continental Congress, the creation of or abandonment of the First and Second Banks of the United States, controlling or encouraging free banking, abandoning the convertibility of gold in the 1860s and returning to the gold standard in the 1870s, the arguments over bimetallism and William Jennings Bryan's Cross of Gold in the 1890s, or how and whether to maintain the gold standard after World War I, returning to the gold standard would not eliminate the political debate, it would just shift the debate to a different set of arguments.

Nevertheless, a majority of elected officials at both the federal and state levels would have to be elected who supported implementing, then maintaining the new gold standard. Of course, this only begs the question because in order for gold-standard politicians to exist, we would need a gold-standard electorate who are willing to vote for politicians who support a new gold standard and against politicians who oppose it. This leads to the final step.

Step 5. Accept the Costs and Consequences of a New Gold Standard

At no point in America's past did everyone support the gold standard. There were always people who were opposed to the gold standard because of the costs of deflation and tight money that come with the gold standard, and there were always those who supported the gold standard for the monetary stability that it provided.

If America wants to return to the gold standard, the electorate needs to ask itself whether it is willing to accept the costs as well as the benefits of returning to the gold standard.

The primary cost is subjugating monetary and fiscal policy to maintaining the gold standard and accepting the responsibility that goes along with that decision because there would be real costs. Many of these costs were discussed above. There are no free lunches, even with a gold standard.

For monetary policy, returning to the gold standard means using higher interest rates and deflation as a way of maintaining the fixed price of gold, even during a recession. This also means maintaining the Fed's independence to defend the gold standard against the short-run needs of politicians. If defending the dollar's link to gold means higher unemployment and slower growth, then so be it. Of course, supporters of the new gold standard would argue that in the long run, the monetary benefits of abandoning a fiat currency and maintaining a link to gold would offset these short-run costs, but that is a judgment the United States as a whole would have to make.

For fiscal policy, returning to the gold standard would mean subjugating federal government spending and taxing to maintaining a balanced budget that would enable the United States to maintain the dollar's link to gold. Any deficit in the current fiscal year would need to be offset by surpluses in the future. If unexpected expenses, such as a war occurred, the electorate would have to accept higher taxes. There would have to be caps on "entitlements" such as Social Security, Medicare and Medicaid. This could mean raising the retirement age, cutting Social Security benefits, introducing means testing, requiring more medical co-pays, capping the amount spent by Medicare on any individual or introducing other measures that would limit the amount the government spends on entitlements as a share of GDP. The federal government could no longer bail out the public and private sector. Transfers from the federal government to states and municipalities would have to be severely limited and unfunded emergency requests for funds would have to be ignored. If a corporation or bank was in trouble, they would fail.

If this is what the electorate wants and the United States can put maintaining a gold standard and its benefits above the costs that a new gold standard would incur, then they will elect politicians who will implement these changes. If the electorate feels the cost-benefit tradeoffs of a fiat currency with inflation, large redistributions and transfers through entitlements and bailouts, a depreciating currency, intervention in the economy from fiscal and monetary policy, government deficits, and everything else that comes with a fiat currency is better than the consequences of reintroducing the gold standard, they will stick with the current system. The important thing is that people understand the costs and benefits of each monetary system and choose the one that maximizes the benefits to the majority of people in the country.

Which Came First, the Goose or the Golden Egg?

Did the gold standard produce the fiscal and monetary restraint that occurred during the 1800s, or did the fiscal and monetary restraint of the 1800s enable the gold standard to exist. Which came first, the Goose or the Golden Egg?

Can the United States return to the gold standard? Absolutely. Is the gold standard a relic of the past that can never be reintroduced? No. Are there both costs and benefits of returning to the gold standard? Absolutely. Should we return to the gold standard? That is up to the electorate.

Even if the United States decided to return to the gold standard, it would be difficult for the United States to do so unless other countries joined it. The gold standard was an international system that the largest countries of the world shared. There were alternatives. Countries could adhere to silver, which was more inflationary, or they could temporarily withdraw from the gold standard when war forced the country to use a fiat currency, but the gold standard of the late 1800s grew out of the discovery of new sources for gold which allowed the minting of gold coins and the convertibility of government obligations into gold.

For the United States alone to return to the gold standard while all others continue to use a fiat currency would be chaotic and would probably fail as the United States tried to control the value of gold against the rest of the world. Given the United States' current level of debt, this would prove especially difficult. The United States would need to pay down its debt and build up reserves before it would be able to defend its gold standard against the rest of the world. To say the least, the United States is not currently in that position. For that reason, any return to a gold standard would probably have to be part of an integrated international effort, not the action of a single country.

To actually return to the gold standard, the five steps listed above would have to be taken in reverse order. First, the electorate would have to decide that the gold standard is preferable to a fiat currency, then the electorate would choose politicians who can put the gold standard into place. The politicians would have to pass bills to ensure a balanced budget in the future and change the directive of the Fed to defending the new gold standard. Then once that was in place, they could fix the price of the dollar to gold.

If the government were to enact the first four steps, returning to the gold standard would be a simple matter. In a way, it might even be superfluous. Most people who argue for a return to the gold standard do so because it would constrain the government's ability to use fiscal and monetary policy to manipulate the economy and produce bubbles, but it isn't the introduction of the gold standard which creates stable economic conditions, it is the fiscal and monetary policy needed to maintain the gold standard that provides stability. Despite the benefits of the gold standard during the nineteenth century and its ability to control inflation, as

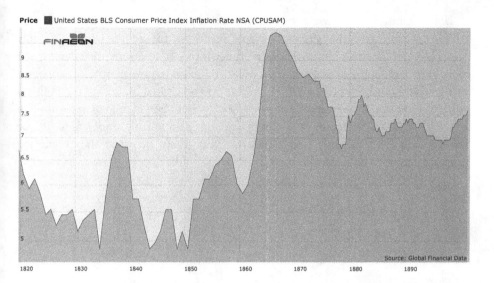

Price ■ United States BLS Consumer Price Index Inflation Rate NSA (CPUSAM)

Figure 2.2 United States Consumer Price Index, 1820 to 1901.

illustrated in Figure 2.2, which illustrates the lack of inflation in the 1800s when the Civil War occurred in the United States or World War I in Europe, countries went off the gold standard because they had to. That would also be the fate of any gold standard in the twenty-first century as well.

To reiterate, it is the constraints the government places on fiscal and monetary policy that enables the government to adhere to the gold standard, not vice versa. Even if linking the U.S. dollar directly to gold in a world where no other country is on the gold standard is difficult to do, there is no reason why the policies needed to maintain a gold standard cannot be introduced or enacted, regardless of whether the country actually reintroduces the gold standard.

The key to maintaining a gold standard without the gold is that there be legal restraints on the government to prevent it from carrying out the inflationary policies of the past few decades. Passing a constitutional amendment to balance the budget or congressionally changing the directive of the Fed might meet this purpose. Nevertheless, some people may feel that only the actual link to gold would ensure stable monetary policies and constraints on government activism.

Both the gold standard and a fiat currency have their costs and benefits. Those who advocate returning to a gold standard rarely describe the consequences and the costs of doing so. Unfortunately, both sides spend more time attacking each other than laying out the trade-offs, costs and benefits of once again making gold the basis of the American economy. Perhaps we haven't reached the point where the electorate feels the costs of a fiat currency are great enough to justify abandoning it for gold.

If the United States were to reintroduce the gold standard in a world in which no other country was on the gold standard, the action would probably fail. Nevertheless, this doesn't prevent the United States from introducing the monetary and financial policies that would be necessary to maintain adherence to a gold standard. The real question is whether the United States has the political will to make these changes. Currently, it does not, but if talk of returning to the gold standard increases, it is important that people fully understand all the repercussions of returning to the gold standard. Only then can they make the political decision required to return to the gold standard.

chapter three

The End of the Gold Standard

It was over 100 years ago, in 1914, that the gold standard died. When World War I began, most countries went off the gold standard and attempts to return to a gold standard since have all failed. Some people have called for a return to the gold standard as a way of ensuring that governments do not inflate their way out of their current fiscal problems. If it were only that easy.

What many people don't understand is that in the long run, the international gold standard was a very brief phenomenon, and the fact that the world moved to a gold standard in the late 1800s was primarily a result of the collapse in the relative values of gold and silver. The reality was that Europe was on a bimetallic standard, not a gold standard, from the Middle Ages until the 1800s, and gold triumphed in the nineteenth century because bimetallism had failed.

The Origins of the Gold Standard

The first gold and silver coins were issued by Croesus in Lydia around 600 B.C. Before that, both gold and silver were used as a store of wealth, for conspicuous consumption, and as a medium of exchange, but no coins existed. The value of gold relative to silver, known as the gold/silver ratio, changed over time. In 2700 BC it was around 9 to 1; under Hammurabi in 1800 BC it was 6 to 1; and by the time Croesus issued the first gold and silver coins, rather than electrum coins made of both gold and silver, it was 12 to 1.

The gold/silver ratio remained around 12 to 1 for the next 2,500 years, though it could range as low as 9 to 1 or as high as 16 to 1. Athens built its empire on the silver mines of Laurium; Alexander the Great plundered the treasuries of the Persians for gold; and the Romans seized stolen bullion from the countries they conquered. Constantine took the gold of the pagan temples for his needs, and whoever controlled Egypt could rely upon the mines in Nubia as a source of gold. When the Arabs spread Islam through the world, they seized the gold and silver of the lands they conquered. When the Arabs gained control over northern Africa, they also gained power over the gold coming from sub-Saharan Africa.

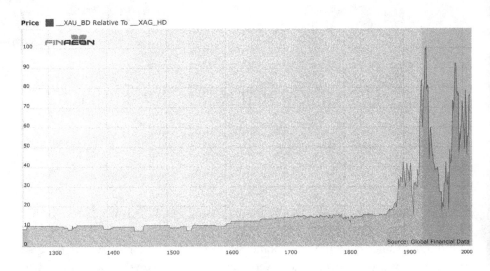

Figure 3.1 Price of Gold Relative to Silver in London, 1257 to 2012.

Europeans minted a few gold coins during their Dark Ages, but mainly they relied upon Arab gold coins. It wasn't until the Europeans sacked Constantinople during the Crusades, taking its gold, and the Venetian cities developed trade surpluses with the Arabs that Europe found a need to mint gold on a regular basis, starting in 1252.

In the thirteenth century, the gold to silver ratio was around 10 to 1. Few realize it was the scarcity of gold in the fifteenth century that drove the Portuguese to go south and east to seek gold and silver, and the Spaniards to go west, across the Atlantic, discovering the Americas instead of reaching China.

The discovery of America released not only the gold of the Americas, which the Spaniards seized, but the silver of Potosí and Mexico, which supplemented the silver mines of Germany that were producing silver Thalers. Galleons filled with silver from the Americas crossed the oceans to Europe and China every year during the 1600s, causing global inflation in the seventeenth century.

Figure 3.1, which uses the gold/silver ratio for the United Kingdom through 1800 and the United States after 1800, shows that between 1250 and 1850, the value of gold relative to silver gradually increased, rising from around 10 to 1 in 1250 to 15 to 1 around 1850, but remained relatively stable. Despite all the discoveries of gold and silver, the seizure of gold and silver by conquerors from the conquered, or the changes in the global economy during those intervening 600 years, the ratio of the price of gold to silver saw no dramatic changes.

This stability enabled the bimetallic standard to prevail for those 600 years. As one country changed the domestic ratio of gold to silver, gold would leave one country and flow into the other. If the gold/silver ratio was 12 in France and 11.5 in the Netherlands, gold would flow to France, where it was more highly valued, and silver would flow to the Netherlands. If the Netherlands changed the ratio to 12.5 to 1, gold would flow from France to the Netherlands.

Government has a long history of debasing the currency. Paper money only enabled governments to speed up the process of debasement. The English silver shilling had 16.2 grams of silver under William I in 1066, but only 2.6 grams under Henry VIII in 1546. The French livre tournois had 84 grams of gold under Philip Augustus II in 1200, but only 4.5 grams when the French Revolution began in 1789. The worst European offender was Spain, whose maravedí had 52 grams of silver in 1200, but only 0.031 grams of silver in 1808. This means coins were debased by a factor of 150 in Spain.

Gold Triumphs

What happened in the 1800s to change the gold/silver ratio forever? There were new discoveries of gold in California, Australia, South Africa and the Yukon, but also huge discoveries of silver in Nevada and Colorado. This caused a collapse in the price of silver, as well as its price relative to gold, as Figure 3.2 shows.

Countries did not move to the gold standard because it was the right thing to do, but because the collapse in the price of silver made silver a token commodity. The relationship between gold and silver that had held for 600 years was irrevocably broken. Although almost every developed country was on the gold standard by

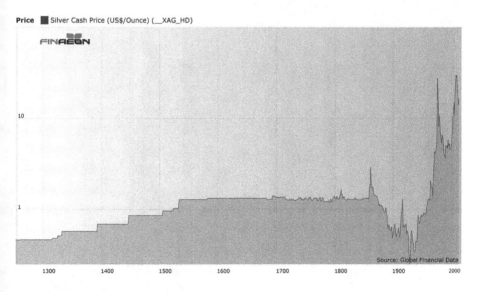

Figure 3.2 Price of Silver, 1257 to 2012.

1900, few realized it was the lull before the storm. When World War I broke out in August 1914, the gold standard was dead.

Attempts to resurrect the gold standard after World War I, after World War II and today were doomed to fail because the relationship between gold and silver has changed forever. Could a country like the United States return to a gold standard? In theory, yes as demonstrated in Chapter Two. In practice, it is highly unlikely.

Beginning in the 1870s, new discoveries of silver reduced its value to the point that it could no longer be used as the primary medium of exchange for an economy. The gold/silver ratio became so volatile that the bimetallism the world had operated under for centuries was no longer viable. Bank money became the alternative to gold, not silver. This remains true today, and will remain true in the future.

part two

Inflation: Money as a Weapon of Mass Destruction

chapter four

A Century of Inflation

The twentieth century will be remembered as a century of excess. In every area, more things were done in the twentieth century than in any other century in history, and in many cases, more than in all of the previous centuries combined. The twentieth century saw some of the most destructive wars in history, the development of the atomic bomb, the beginning of air and space travel, the colonization and decolonization of the Third World, the rise and fall of communism, dramatic improvements in the standard of living, the population explosion, the rise of the computer, incredible advances in science and medicine, and hundreds of historically unprecedented changes.

The twentieth century also produced more inflation than any other century in history. Inflation is nothing new. Roman rulers produced inflation in third-century Rome by debasing their coins; China suffered inflation in the fourteenth century when the emperors replaced coins with paper money; Europe and the rest of the world suffered inflation when gold and silver started flowing into the Old World from the New World in the sixteenth century; and the French and Americans endured severe inflation to fund their revolutions.

Nevertheless, as we shall see, the twentieth century produced the worst inflation in human history. Every single country in the world suffered worse inflation in the twentieth century than in any century in history. What caused this inflation to occur? Will the twenty-first century bear high inflation as well?

The Nineteenth Century

Amazingly enough, the nineteenth century was a period of deflation, rather than inflation. From the end of the Napoleonic Wars in 1815 until the start of World War II in 1914, there was no inflation in most countries, and in some cases, prices were lower in 1914 than they had been in 1815. Prices fluctuated up and down from one decade to the next, but overall, prices remained stable.

There were exceptions to this rule. The United States suffered inflation during the Civil War, though the United States experienced deflation after the war in order to bring the economy back onto the gold standard. The Confederate states suffered high inflation because they printed money to pay for the war. The eventual collapse of the Confederate states made their currency worthless.

Countries were able to minimize the amount of inflation they suffered during the nineteenth century because currencies were tied to commodities (gold and silver), whose supply increased at rates similar to the increase in output. Price stability in gold and silver produced price stability for the world.

The nineteenth century was a period of bimetallism. Countries chose to back their currency with either gold or silver. The United Kingdom was on the gold standard from the end of the Napoleonic Wars until 1914. Because the British economy grew faster than the supply of gold, prices fell in Britain during that hundred-year period.

Other countries such as France, Russia, Austria and most countries of Asia tied their currency to silver. Because the supply of silver was growing faster than the supply of gold, countries on a silver standard had higher inflation rates than countries on the gold standard. Nevertheless, their inflation was modest by twentieth-century standards.

Other countries such as the United States, primarily for political reasons, tried to balance themselves between gold and silver by tying their currency to both metals, but in the end, gold triumphed. By the beginning of the twentieth century, every major country in the world had tied its currency to gold.

The result was a century of price and currency stability. The value of the U.S. dollar relative to the British pound sterling was the same in 1914 as it had been in 1830. Because currencies were tied to gold, fluctuations in exchange rates were minimal, rarely moving more than 1 percent above or below par. Given this situation, nothing could have prepared the world for the hyperinflations and persistent inflation of the twentieth century.

Why will the twentieth century be remembered as the century of the worst inflation in human history? How did the twentieth century differ from the nineteenth century? Which countries suffered the worst inflation, and why? Which countries suffered the least inflation, and why? And most importantly, will the twenty-first century be another century of inflation? Or will the world enjoy a century of price and financial stability similar to what occurred during the nineteenth century?

Exchange Rates and Inflation

It would have been easy to write this chapter if every country had kept data on inflation throughout the twentieth century. Unfortunately, this isn't the case. Most countries only began keeping data on inflation after World War I, and for smaller countries, data often does not exist before World War II. Inflation data before these dates are often estimates using historical price data.

The worst inflationary periods often lack any inflationary data at all. It is easy to keep track of inflation when prices are rising at 2 percent per annum, but more difficult when prices are doubling on a daily basis, as happened in Germany in the 1920s, Hungary in the 1940s and in Yugoslavia in the 1990s. In order to compare inflation throughout the world, we have had to rely upon a proxy for inflation: exchange rates.

The theory of purchasing power parity says that in the long run, differences in inflation rates between countries are transmitted through changes in relative exchange rates. If prices double in one country but remain unchanged in another country, the currency of the inflating country will lose half of its value relative to the currency of the stable country. Otherwise, exports from the inflating country would become so expensive that foreigners could not afford to purchase their exports. For this reason, all inflation comparisons will be based upon exchange rate changes over time.

Inflation in the Twentieth Century

A complete consumer price inflation record is available for the United Kingdom during the entire nineteenth century. Prices in the United Kingdom rose during the Napoleonic Wars, and started to decline after 1813, returning to stable pre-war levels by 1822. From 1822 until 1912, consumer prices showed no overall increase. There were periods of moderate inflation and deflation, but no overall inflationary trend. This general pattern holds true for other countries for which inflation data are available.

The twentieth century is quite another matter. Whereas the nineteenth century went through periods of moderate inflation and deflation, the twentieth century was a period of continual inflation, with some periods worse than others. The only times in which prices fell were the periods right after World War I and the Depression of the 1930s. During all other periods, prices generally rose.

Table 4.1 compares the inflation experiences of the United Kingdom and the United States between 1820 and 2000, providing both the index for each country and the annual inflation rates during the 20-year and 10-year periods that are covered. Several facts are immediately obvious.

First, the lack of inflation in the nineteenth century is clearly visible. Even in the United States during the 1860 to 1880 period when the Civil War occurred, the overall level of inflation was lower than in most of the post-World War II era. Second, both the United States and the United Kingdom had similar inflation experiences throughout the nineteenth century. By contrast, not only was inflation higher in the twentieth century in the United States and the United Kingdom, but it was also more variable, both within and between countries. Greater inflation in the United Kingdom in the 1910s led to greater deflation in the 1920s than in

Table 4.1 Inflation in the United Kingdom and United States

Years	United Kingdom Annual Inflation Rate	United States Annual Inflation Rate
1800–1820	0.99	1.00
1820–1840	–0.25	–0.30
1840–1860	0.11	0.09
1860–1880	–0.54	1.46
1880–1900	–0.76	–0.07
1900–1910	0.53	2.26
1910–1920	10.67	7.62
1920–1930	–5.34	–1.85
1930–1940	2.50	–1.32
1940–1950	1.78	5.89
1950–1960	3.27	1.77
1960–1970	4.27	2.94
1970–1980	13.79	8.05
1980–1990	6.39	4.48
1990–2000	2.86	2.66
2000–2010	2.86	2.34

the United States. The same was not true after the war. The United Kingdom had greater inflation than the United States in every decade after 1950.

Table 4.1 also shows the merits of using purchasing power parity to analyze inflationary differences between countries. Whereas wholesale prices in the United States increased 14-fold in the twentieth century, wholesale prices increased 53-fold in the United Kingdom. Prices rose 3.75 times faster in the United Kingdom than in the United States during the twentieth century. For this reason, the British pound should have depreciated from 4.85 dollars to the pound in 1900 to 1.30 dollars to the pound in 2000, which is not far from the actual rate of about 1.45 pounds to the dollar.

A Brief History of Inflation in the Twentieth Century

The review of inflation in the United Kingdom and the United States showed that inflation varied from one decade to the next. Inflation in the twentieth century can be divided into a number of periods of deflation and inflation. Economic and political events were the primary factors that set the tone for each of these periods. We divide the inflationary experience of the twentieth century into seven periods:

Years	Economic Period
1900–1914	The gold standard and stability
1915–1924	World War I and inflation
1925–1939	Interwar instability and deflation
1939–1949	World War II, monetary controls and post-war inflation
1949–1970	Bretton Woods and the dollar standard, moderate inflation
1971–1979	Floating exchange rates, OPEC and highly variable inflation
1980–2000	Greater central bank independence and disinflation

The first period lasted from 1900 until August 1914. This was a period of relative price stability. All major European countries, and many non-European countries, were on the gold standard. Weaker economies tied their currency to silver. During this period, there was modest inflation throughout the world, and a large degree of stability in foreign exchange markets between currencies.

The next period, from 1914 until 1924, was a period of instability, inflation and hyperinflation. Within days of the outbreak of World War I, all the countries involved had left the gold standard. Unable to finance the war through taxes alone, countries resorted to printing excessive amounts of money to pay for the war. The result was the highest inflation the world had experienced since the Napoleonic Wars. The overall price level more than doubled in every country involved in the war.

The period immediately after World War I produced even worse inflation than during the war for many countries. Countries that were victorious in World War I, such as the United Kingdom and the United States, deflated after 1920, but countries that had been defeated faced political instability after the war and underwent some of the worst hyperinflations in human history.

Post-War Inflation Explodes

New countries that were created after the war, such as Poland and Hungary, lacked the ability to collect sufficient taxes and paid their bills by printing money. Revolutions rocked Russia and other countries, war indemnities had to be paid by Germany, governments faced new demands for government services and were burdened with debt from the war. These and other problems made inflation an attractive alternative to cutting services or raising taxes in many of the European

Table 4.2 U.S. Dollar Exchange Rates in 1914 and 1924

Country	1914	1924
Austria	4.96	71,428
Germany	4.2	4,200,000,000,000
Hungary	4.96	77,000
Poland	5.3*	9,330,000
Russia	2.35	257,500,000,000

* Poland Markka rates are for 1916

countries that had been directly involved in World War I. This solution only created more economic problems. The result was hyperinflation in Germany and other countries that had been fighting on the side of the Axis powers, or had been occupied by the Axis powers. Table 4.2 illustrates the dramatic changes in U.S. dollar exchnge rates between 1914 and 1924 for some of these countries.

The period from 1924 until 1939 was one of financial instability and deflation. By 1924, most countries, including Germany, had stabilized. The driving force behind the financial system during the interwar period was the attempt to return to the stability of the pre-war gold standard. After ending its hyperinflation, Germany exchanged 1,000,000,000,000 marks for 1 Rentenmark, and set the exchange rate for the Rentenmark equal to the pre-World War I rate for the mark. Britain put the pound sterling back on its pre-war gold parity, and other countries tried to do the same. Instead of returning to economic growth and stability, each country sank into economic depression, accompanied by deflation.

Between 1939 and 1949, most countries avoided the inflation of World War I by introducing price controls. Governments also used exchange rate controls to limit access to foreign exchange, effectively freezing exchange rates during the war. After the war, inflation set in, and the countries that had been devastated by World War II suffered inflation or hyperinflation. As is shown in Table 4.3, China, Hungary, Greece, Romania and others went through hyperinflations after World War II even worse than the inflations that followed World War I.

Table 4.3 U.S. Dollar Exchange Rates in 1939 and 1949

Country	1939	1949
China	17.5	1,275,000,000,000,000
Greece	140	500,000,000,000,000
Hungary	5	4,700,000,000,000,000,000,000
Romania	142	3,000,000

The period from 1949 until 1973 was the Bretton Woods era. A realignment of currencies in September 1949, which allowed most currencies to initially depreciate against the dollar, created the basis for 25 years of currency stability. Though exchange rates were stable, prices were not. The dollar played the role of the world's reserve currency during the third quarter of the twentieth century, just as the British pound had played this role in the nineteenth century. However, the United States preferred moderate inflation to the possibility of returning to the high unemployment and deflation of the 1930s.

The nineteenth century avoided inflation by tying the financial system to gold. The increase in the supply of gold was less than the increase in the supply of goods in general, so inflation was avoided. By tying all the world's currencies to the U.S. dollar, the United States had responsibility for maintaining a stable currency, and in this, the United States failed. Between 1949 and 1974, consumer prices in the United States doubled, and consequently, the prices of goods in all countries increased twofold or more.

During the late 1960s and early 1970s, there were strains on the Bretton Woods system. The scarcity of dollars in the 1950s had turned into a surfeit by 1970. Because currencies were tied to the dollar, and each country had a separate currency and central bank, countries suffered different rates of inflation. The exchange rates that had been established in 1949 lost their validity, as countries began suffering different rates of inflation, trade patterns changed, and international capital flows increased. In August 1971, the United States devalued the dollar, and by 1973, most of the world's major currencies were floating against one another. Table 4.4 follows the evolution of exchange rates between the world's major currencies during the period from 1939 to 1979.

After countries began floating their currencies in 1973, the OPEC oil crisis hit, producing an inflation-inducing supply shock that lasted for the rest of the decade.

Table 4.4 U.S. Dollar Exchange Rates in 1939, 1949 and 1979

Country	1939	1949	1979
France*	0.45	3.495	4.02
Germany*	0.25	4.2	1.73
Italy	19	620	800
Japan	4.27	360	240
Switzerland	4.46	4.3	1.6
United Kingdom	0.25	0.357	0.45

* Exchange rates for the French franc and German mark have been adjusted for currency changes.

Most countries suffered the worst peacetime inflation in their history. Governments thought they would avoid unemployment through monetary accommodation during the 1970s, but when the second oil shock hit in 1979, central banks saw that during the 1970s, unemployment had risen and growth had declined while inflation got worse. Inflation in developed countries hit double digits, and inflation in developing countries often hit triple digits. There were few hyperinflations in the 1970s, but many countries suffered continuous high rates of inflation resulting from monetary accommodation. Former European colonies that had anchored their financial system to European currencies after independence gradually broke the link, eliminating their inflationary discipline. Countries in Africa and Latin America suffered unprecedented rates of inflation.

When Paul Volcker became chairman of the Federal Reserve in 1979, he decided to fight inflation even if the cost was higher unemployment. This determination, along with the weakening of OPEC after 1981, led to a decade of disinflation in the 1980s, and low and moderate inflation in the 1990s. When the governments in Eastern Europe and the Soviet Union collapsed in the early 1990s, many of these countries suffered hyperinflation when they tried to adjust to a market economy; however, the rest of the world saw decreasing rates of inflation. Even African and Latin American countries that had suffered high rates of inflation throughout the post-World War II period learned to tame inflation. Argentina, for example, reduced inflation by introducing a currency board and linking their currency to the dollar.

At this point, one would expect that the twenty-first century should be a century of low inflation similar to what occurred during the Bretton Woods period between 1949 and 1969. But this isn't certain. Several countries, such as Japan and Singapore, actually went through deflation in the 1990s, and there is always the risk that economic and political instability in the twenty-first century will cause inflations similar to what happened during the Napoleonic Wars, World War I and World War II. No one knows what will happen in the century to come, but we can learn lessons from the last century.

Appreciating Countries

Although prices in the United States increased 23-fold in the twentieth century, most countries suffered even worse inflation than the United States. Since inflation data are incomplete, we make our comparisons by looking at exchange rate changes during the twentieth century.

You can literally count on your hand the number of countries whose currencies appreciated against the dollar in the twentieth century, and only one currency, the Swiss franc, appreciated significantly. This means that with a few exceptions, the United States had the best inflation record of any country in the world during the twentieth century.

Table 4.5 U.S. Dollar Exchange Rates 1900 to 2000

	Netherlands	Netherlands Antilles	Singapore	Switzerland
1900	2.48	2.48	1.93	5.19
1920	3.23	3.23	2.47	6.49
1940	1.87	1.87	2.12	4.31
1960	3.77	1.87	3.12	4.31
1980	2.15	1.79	2.09	1.79
2000	2.34	1.78	1.73	1.61

Table 4.5 shows the only countries whose currencies appreciated against the U.S. dollar during the twentieth century. Two other currencies should also be mentioned. The Aruba florin, which was created in 1986 when Aruba separated from the Netherlands Antilles, had a similar exchange rate history to the Netherlands Antilles, and Brunei Darussalam, which has pegged its currency to the Straits Settlement/Singapore dollar giving it a currency history similar to that of Singapore.

Switzerland had the least inflation of any country in the twentieth century. Prices increased tenfold between 1900 and 2000. At any point in time, Switzerland's inflationary history was similar to that of the rest of the world, but its actual inflation rates were lower. Switzerland suffered inflation between 1915 and 1920, deflation between 1920 and 1936, and gradual inflation thereafter.

Switzerland has followed an explicit policy of minimizing inflation. The Swiss National Bank is independent of government influence, and because of Switzerland's role as an important international finance center, maintaining a strong currency has been important. Had Switzerland allowed its currency to depreciate, it would have lost its role as a safe haven for funds. Moreover, Switzerland is a federation that lacks a strong central government, and it avoided participation in either of the European World Wars. Switzerland avoided the economic and political chaos that usually accompanies inflation, avoided high government deficits, avoided large increases in government spending and provided the Swiss National Bank with independence. Because Switzerland has been a small, open country, it has had to focus on maintaining a strong, liquid currency. For this reason, the Swiss franc was the world's strongest currency in the twentieth century.

The Netherlands is also a small, open economy with a long, commercial history. The country was neutral in World War I, but was invaded during World War II. Although it is more centralized, and has a larger role for government and social spending than Switzerland, it has avoided the economic and political problems that often plunge countries into inflation. Consumer prices rose 24-fold in the Netherlands during the twentieth century, almost exactly the same as in the United States, which is why the currencies were almost unchanged against each other during the twentieth century. Of course, the Netherlands has forsaken the guilder, introducing the euro in

1999. The European central bank will run the Netherlands' monetary policy in the twenty-first century as long as the Netherlands is part of the euro.

The Netherlands Antilles benefited from linking its currency to the Netherlands from 1900 until 1940 and to the United States from 1940 until 2000. Aruba became a separate country in 1986 and introduced the Florin at par with the Netherlands Antilles guilder. The Netherlands Antilles is still part of the Netherlands, and it has never pursued an independent monetary policy. There can be no other explanation for its inflationary record.

By contrast, Suriname, which was a Dutch dependency until it gained its independence in 1976, capitulated to the temptations of inflation. The Suriname and Antillean guilders were at par to one another until the 1960s, but by 2000, it took 550 Suriname guilders to get one Antillean guilder. Sometimes, a lack of independence can be a blessing in disguise.

The final currency that appreciated against the U.S. dollar was the Singapore dollar. The Singapore dollar is a successor to the Straits Settlements dollar, Malayan dollar and Malaysian ringgit. Brunei linked its currency to the Singapore dollar throughout the twentieth century, and its currency has mirrored the behavior of the Singapore dollar.

Singapore is in a situation similar to Switzerland. It is a small, open economy, dependent on trade, and has maintained a steady currency as a result. The Singapore dollar was linked to the British pound between 1905 and 1970. Since 1970, the Singapore Monetary Authority has controlled inflation, causing the Singapore dollar to appreciate by 55 percent against the U.S. dollar. Throughout most of its history, the Straits Settlements/Singapore used a currency board to maintain its stable currency. Prices in Singapore rose only fourfold after World War II, which is why the currency remained so strong. Brunei maintained a strong currency, in part, because of its oil wealth.

This leaves us with the question: why did these countries—Switzerland, Netherlands Antilles/Aruba, the Netherlands and Singapore/Brunei—succeed in controlling inflation during the twentieth century when other countries failed? We believe the most important factors were:

1. All the countries had small, open economies dependent on trade.
2. They all had independent monetary authorities or currency boards that avoided an overissue of currency.
3. None of these countries suffered periods of economic or political chaos that might have led to high rates of inflation, even though both the Netherlands and Singapore were occupied during World War II.
4. None of the governments have used large government deficits to fund social and defense programs that could have produced inflation. Although the Netherlands suffered from the "Dutch Disease" in the 1970s, when it used its oil revenues to fund generous social programs, it has since reformed itself and reduced social benefits.

The paradox of fighting inflation is that the best way to control inflation is to minimize control over monetary policy. Large countries should rely upon an independent central bank, dedicated to fighting inflation, and small countries should use a currency board, or some other means, to import the monetary policy of a country with anti-inflationary policies. Politics influences economic policy, and minimizing this link is one of the best ways of fighting inflation.

High-Inflation Countries

Countries that suffered the highest rates of inflation in the twentieth century endured one or more bouts of hyperinflation, went through decades of high inflation rates, or both. The German economy, for example, almost collapsed in 1923 as a result of hyperinflation in which a meal costing 1 mark at the beginning of World War I cost 1 trillion marks by the end of 1923. Brazil, on the other hand, had inflation rates of over 10 percent every year from 1951 to 1995, and over 1,000 percent in some years, but never sank into hyperinflation. The cumulative effect over the decades was a complete and steady devaluation in the various currencies that Brazil issued. The country with the worst inflation record in the twentieth century, Yugoslavia, suffered both types of inflation: double-digit inflation during most of the 1960s, all of the 1970s and 1980s, and a collapse into hyperinflation in the early 1990s.

Table 4.6 lists the countries with the worst inflation in the twentieth century by showing how many units of its year 2000 currency was needed to purchase the equivalent of one U. S. dollar in 1900 For example, since it took 2 Japanese yen to purchase 1 U.S. dollar in 1900, and 114 yen in 2000, the depreciation factor for the Japanese yen would be 57. The equivalent amounts for the countries listed in the table are mind-boggling.

Rather than provide histories of each country, it would be easier to look at the factors that caused these countries to suffer inflation as some of the same causes apply to several countries.

From a geographic point of view, there are several interesting things to note. First, the only Asian country in the list is China, primarily because of the hyperinflation it fell into during the last years of the nationalist regime in China. No other Asian country went through hyperinflationary periods in the twentieth century, though countries like Indonesia suffered high rates of inflation at different points in time.

Second, several South American countries are included in the list, but with the exception of Nicaragua no Central American or North American countries are represented. Central American countries kept their currencies linked to the U.S. dollar during most of the century, minimizing their currencies' depreciation and their domestic inflation. Many South American countries, on the other hand, suffered both continuous high rates of inflation and periods of hyperinflation.

Table 4.6 Countries with the Greatest
Depreciation against the Dollar, 1900 to 2000

Country	Depreciation Factor
Yugoslavia	5.34×10^{30}
Hungary	2.83×10^{26}
Russia	7.16×10^{16}
China	2.00×10^{16}
Congo (Zaire)	2.90×10^{15}
Brazil	1.11×10^{15}
Germany	4.94×10^{12}
Argentina	1.00×10^{11}
Nicaragua	6.45×10^{10}
Angola	1.26×10^{10}
Bolivia	2.47×10^{9}
Peru	1.75×10^{9}
Chile	1.98×10^{8}
Poland	1.77×10^{8}

Unlike Central American countries, they pursued independent monetary policies and suffered as a result. South American countries, in general, had higher average inflation rates than the rest of the world throughout the twentieth century.

Third, European countries on this list mainly went through a period of hyperinflation either after World War I, World War II, or the collapse of the Soviet Union. During most other time periods, inflation rates were moderate.

Finally, only two African countries are on the list. Most African colonies had currency boards until the 1960s that limited inflation by tying their currency to European currencies. The French West African countries that still tie their currency to the French franc/euro have suffered significantly less inflation than the countries that have chosen independent monetary policies. Congo's inflation occurred under the despotic Mobutu, and Angola's inflation occurred almost exclusively during the 1990s.

As the monetary dictum goes, inflation is everywhere a monetary phenomenon. This rule is especially true in these cases. Every one of the countries listed in Table 4.6 was unable and/or unwilling to pay for government expenditures through raising taxes. Each chose to print money, through excessive issues of currency or open market operations, increasing the money supply and causing inflation.

Over time, this action became a self-defeating measure as inflation reduced real government receipts making the deficit even larger until their economy collapsed into hyperinflation.

We divide our sources of hyperinflation into four categories: post-World War I inflation, post-World War II inflation, post-Soviet Union inflation, and inflationary financing of government deficits leading to a collapse in the currency.

Post-World War I Inflation

After World War I, the Axis countries that were defeated in the war were in political and financial disarray. Austria-Hungary broke up into several smaller countries, Poland was reborn, Russia collapsed into civil war, and Germany and other countries fell under severe economic pressures. These countries gradually fell into a vicious circle of government deficits that led to inflation, which fed the demand for more government services as economic recession set in, leading to even greater inflation. In Poland, Germany, Hungary, Russia and Austria, the government eventually replaced the collapsed paper currencies with new currencies, tying the new currencies to the U.S. dollar, gold or some other anchor. Germany's inflation was the worst, and Germany has been hypervigilant against inflation ever since. Though Germany and Austria never suffered high rates of inflation again, Hungary suffered the worst inflation in history after World War II, and both Poland and Russia suffered inflationary bouts after Communism collapsed in each country.

None of the Allied countries suffered hyperinflation after World War I. Prices in most countries had doubled, tripled or quadrupled during World War I, but after the war deflation set in. The United Kingdom and other countries tried to return to the gold standard, reestablishing the exchange rates that had existed prior to World War I.

Political and economic collapse was the clear source of inflation after the war. Countries such as Germany and Austria that chose to inflate, rather than address their economic problems directly, discovered the costs of hyperinflation and have made sure that hyperinflation never occurred again. Other countries, such as Hungary or Romania were unable to avoid inflation and suffered as a result.

Post-World War II Inflation

Fewer countries suffered from inflation after World War II than after World War I. China's inflationary collapse had more to do with the civil war that followed World War II than with the war itself. The Communist parts of China had much lower inflation rates during the Civil War than the Nationalist parts of China. The Communist yuan fell in value form 3.9 yuan to the dollar in 1934 to 47,000 by 1949, but the nationalist yuan fell in value to 425,000,000 yuan to the dollar. Greece suffered its inflation during World War II, and Romania's inflation was moderate compared to the inflation in Hungary.

The worst inflation in human history occurred in Hungary in 1946 when the pengö drowned in zeroes. During the spring and summer of 1946, Hungary went through the pengö , milpengö (equal to 1 million pengö), bilpengö (equal to 1 million million pengö) and adopengö (the "tax" pengö, which indexed its value to the inflation rate). When the inflation ended in July 1946, it took 400 quadrillion (400,000,000,000,000,000,000) pengö to purchase 1 forint, the new currency. This inflation was in no way inevitable.

Since other East European countries were in similar economic situations, it should be recognized that poor economic policies created Hungary's hyperinflation, not the events themselves. The fact that Taiwan and Communist China suffered much lower inflation rates than Nationalist China shows that the degree of inflation was a political choice. These countries suffered inflation because they were unwilling to deal with the economic problems they were facing.

Post-Soviet Union Inflation

The collapse of the Soviet Union led to hyperinflations in many of the countries that made up the former Soviet Union and other Eastern European countries. Almost every country that was a member of the Soviet Union has had to introduce a new currency to replace the depreciated currencies that immediately followed the Soviet Ruble. The degree of inflation varied from moderate inflation in the Baltic States and Central Asian Republics to hyperinflation in the Slavic countries. Table 4.7 shows some of the worst cases.

The worst inflation occurred in Yugoslavia, primarily during 1993 when the country was under international sanctions and chose to pay its bills through

Table 4.7 U.S. Dollar Exchange Rates in 1989 and 2000

	1989	2000
Belarus	0.746	12,125,000
Georgia	0.746	1,980,000
Poland	507	41,280
Romania	14	25,910
Russia	0.746	28,550
Ukraine	0.746	543,440
Yugoslavia	1.5	661,000,000,000,000,000,000,000

inflationary finance. As a result, Yugoslavia joined Hungary in sharing the record for worst inflations in history. Yugoslavia introduced a new version of the dinar in October 1993, and two new versions of the dinar in January 1994. By the end of January 1994, one "super" dinar could buy 13 trillion billion dinars from September 1993!

Czechoslovakia

One of the most interesting case histories for inflation in the twentieth century is Czechoslovakia/the Czech Republic. Czechoslovakia could have collapsed into hyperinflation following World War I, World War II or the collapse of Communism, but maintained relative price stability in each of these cases. Czechoslovakia went through only one currency reform during the twentieth century, in 1953, when 10 old Czech koruna were exchanged for 1 new Czech koruna. Whereas it took the equivalent of 0.5 new Czech koruna to get a U.S. dollar in 1900, it took 37 Czech koruna in 2000. This certainly was a large depreciation, but nothing compared to the depreciation of any of its neighbors. This underlines the fact that inflation and hyperinflation are a choice.

Inflationary Finance and Currency Collapse

Many of the other countries that suffered severe depreciation of their currency during the twentieth century accomplished this feat through hard and steady work. No South American country faced the political problems caused by the world wars or the collapse of Communism, but all of them suffered high rates of inflation throughout the twentieth century.

The source of this inflation was the unwillingness of governments to balance their books and avoid deficits. Government deficits were paid for with expansions in the money supply, which generated inflation. Argentina, Brazil, Uruguay and other South American countries suffered year after year of double-digit inflation that inevitably led to a collapse of the currency into triple- or quadruple-digit inflation before economic reforms replaced the currency with a new currency. Then the country began a new adventure down the road to inflationary collapse. Brazil went through five currency reforms in the twentieth century; Argentina three reforms; Bolivia, Chile, Nicaragua, Peru and Uruguay two reforms each.

This inflation was in no way inevitable. Panama tied its currency to the U.S. dollar throughout the twentieth century and suffered no depreciation. Most Central American countries tied their currencies to the U.S. dollar until the 1970s and avoided inflation. Although it is difficult to separate the causes and effects of inflation, it is notable that Argentina was richer than most European countries in the 1920s, but is now poorer than most European countries. Latin American countries had slower growth than most Asian countries. Although inflation in and of itself did not cause this result, it certainly contributed to it.

Many countries not on our list have suffered high annual inflation rates without collapsing into hyperinflation. Countries suffer inflation because they are unwilling to deal directly with the economic problems that create inflation. Using the printing press to avoid these problems only delays the inevitable and worsens the economic costs of dealing with inflation.

The Costs of Inflation

Inflation reduces economic well-being. There are numerous economic costs of inflation. Price inflation imposes menu costs (the cost of changing prices), shoe leather costs (the costs of reducing monetary holdings), increased uncertainty among producers and consumers trying to determine the real costs of goods and services, tax distortions and the cost of adjusting to unexpected changes in inflation. Unexpected inflation redistributes money from creditors to debtors and from employees to employers. In the case of hyperinflation, it can easily wipe out the value of financial assets. This leads to reduced investment and lower economic growth. Variable inflation rates create uncertainty that affects the level of economic output.

All of these inflationary problems result from price inflation of goods and services. Another inflationary problem that is often ignored is asset-price inflation in the stock market, real estate market, or other asset markets. Asset inflation creates artificial wealth, encouraging firms and consumers to borrow beyond their capacity. When the asset inflation ends, firms and individuals are unable to pay their debts leading to declines in demand and to economic slowdowns. The United States in the 1930s and Japan in the 1990s are examples of this problem. Asset inflation is deceptive because people feel wealthier when it occurs, but when asset values get out of line with the nation's productive capacity, there will be an inevitable period of "catch up" in which asset prices adjust downward to their real levels.

Both price and asset inflation have their costs.

Fighting Inflation in the Twenty-First Century

Will inflation in the twenty-first century be more like the nineteenth century or the twentieth century? Of course, it is impossible to predict this. Inevitably, countries that choose not to deal with their underlying economic problems will create inflationary problems for themselves. Most countries returned to single-digit levels of inflation in the late 1990s, even South American and former Soviet countries.

Nevertheless, countries do learn from their mistakes. Germany has made sure that it never repeated the hyperinflation of the 1920s, most governments chose to control inflation during World War II and avoid the inflationary finance of World War I, and when the second Oil Crisis occurred in 1979, central banks chose to fight inflation rather than succumbing to it as they had after the first oil crisis in 1973. After the inflation of the Napoleonic Wars, the United States, United Kingdom, France and other countries made sure that paper money inflation did not return for a century. Hence, there is no reason why we cannot use the lessons of the twentieth century to fight inflation in the twenty-first century.

Several conclusions can be made.

1. **Inflation is not the inevitable consequence of political and economic uncertainty.**

Although most countries that suffered inflation did so during a period of political and economic uncertainty, inflation occurred because governments were unwilling to deal with the economic problems they faced. Germany and Austria avoided inflation after World War II, and Czechoslovakia avoided the high inflation rates of its neighbors throughout the twentieth century. Central American countries that tied their currency to the U.S. dollar avoided the inflationary problems of their South American neighbors. Inflation is a choice.

Government and central banks must learn that the economic problems that lead to inflationary finance must be dealt with immediately. Inflation only delays and worsens these economic problems at the cost of economic investment and output.

2. **Independent central banks can reduce the temptation of inflation.**

The countries with the best records on inflation in the twentieth century were also the countries that had independent central banks. Of course, this in and of itself is no guarantee of avoiding inflation. Though Switzerland, the United States and Germany suffered less inflation than most countries after World War II, they still went through brief periods of double-digit inflation. The central bank must have a commitment to fighting inflation at all costs.

The European Central Bank will provide an interesting case study in the twenty-first century. Unlike the Federal Reserve, it is a supranational central bank, controlling the money supply of several sovereign countries. There are other supranational central banks that control the money supply for several countries, such as the East Caribbean Central Bank or the *Banque Centrale des Etats de l'Afrique de l'Ouest*, but these act more like currency boards than central banks.

Although central banks make fighting inflation their primary goal, it is not their only goal. The Federal Reserve tries to balance fighting inflation against internal and economic stability, and its record on fighting price inflation in the 1970s and asset inflation in the 1990s is less than perfect. Independent central banks and a stronger commitment to fighting inflation can avoid the inflation of the twentieth century.

3. Smaller countries should peg their currency to the euro or dollar to avoid inflation.

The small countries with the best records of avoiding inflation are the countries that have used currency boards or dollarization. This requires them to give up control over the monetary side of their economy.

Currency boards or dollarization in and of themselves do not solve a country's economic problems. Argentina, Mexico, Korea and others used the stability of their currency to borrow excessively in U.S. dollars creating financial and economic problems. A currency board combined with conservative macroeconomic policies is the best way to control inflation in small countries.

This is the best explanation of why African countries suffered little inflation before 1960, but high inflation thereafter, why non-French African countries have suffered higher rates of inflation than French African countries, and why Central America endured less inflation than South America.

Several countries have taken this route. Argentina, Hong Kong and Bulgaria, among others, use or have used currency boards to control inflation. Ecuador dollarized, and the U.S. dollar is legal tender in Panama. This also explains why the Netherlands Antilles has one of the best inflation records in the twentieth century.

For small countries, currency boards can act as the equivalent of an independent central bank and are probably the best solution.

Conclusion

What lies ahead in the twenty-first century? No one knows, of course. There will be wars, governments will collapse, ideologies will gain control over economic common sense, and governments will be tempted to use inflation to solve their economic and financial problems. We must remember that inflation is a choice that can be avoided.

One prediction we would like to make here is that if the twentieth century was a century of the proliferation in currencies, the twenty-first century will be a century that sees a reduction in the number of world currencies. Central banks were a growth industry during the twentieth century. Few countries had a central bank in 1900, and most countries and colonies linked their currencies to one another through the gold standard.

As countries gradually removed gold and silver from their national monetary systems, and replaced them with paper, inflation resulted. The world may never return to the gold standard, but it can return to a world in which most of the world's currencies are linked to several central currencies, such as the dollar or the euro. Whether these reserve currencies return to relative price stability, and can avoid the problems of the twentieth century remains uncertain, but it is a goal to aim for.

chapter five

The Greatest Counterfeiter of All Time

Countries throughout the world issue new banknotes every year that are designed to defeat counterfeiters. Among the devices used to make counterfeiting more difficult are intaglio printing, microprinting, plastic currency, watermarks, security threads, holographic strips, electrotyping, see-through windows, and dozens of other devices that require large financial investments today's counterfeiters simply cannot afford.

As financial payments have become digitized, today's financial crooks have turned to electronic means of getting rich, hacking into computers to secret money into offshore accounts and raiding financial information to enrich themselves. Counterfeiting currency has become relatively less remunerative today, and it no longer is the primary way criminals envision getting rich. If counterfeiting was primarily a crime of the past, one wonders who was the greatest counterfeiter of all time?

Government Counterfeiting

Although governments have done more to destroy their own currencies than all the counterfeiters in the history of mankind combined, the government is not the correct answer. Governments have debased their own currency for millennia. Historical examples of government-induced debasement include:

- The Roman Empire replacing its silver denarii with billon antoniniani;
- The Khans of China creating the first paper inflation in the 1300s;
- The United States making its first currency, the Continental dollar, worthless;
- Germany hyperinflating out of its debts by creating trillions of marks.

In holding governments accountable, we are also not talking about one government counterfeiting the currency of another government as the:

- Barbarians did of the Roman gold aureus;
- British did of Continental dollars and French Assignats during the 1700s;

43

- Germans did of British pounds during World War II in Operation Bernhard;
- United States did of Japan's occupation currency of the Philippines;
- North Koreans did of U.S. dollars, making them one of their principle exports.

Governments have consistently destroyed their own currency and those of other countries without ever being held accountable for their actions the way a counterfeiter is punished.

It is one thing for the government to expand the money supply in order to stimulate the economy and help the unemployed. It is quite another for counterfeiters to do the same—albeit on a much smaller scale—to benefit themselves. Counterfeiters provide competition to the government, and though government officials are applauded when they inflate the economy, counterfeiters are condemned to prison—when they are caught.

A Classy Counterfeiter

Our vote for the greatest counterfeiter of all time goes to Artur Alves dos Reis, whose story was recounted by Murray Teigh Bloom in his fascinating book, *The Man Who Stole Portugal*. Reis was both smart and classy, and his criminal operation reflected these qualities. To my knowledge, Reis put together the most audacious counterfeiting scheme in history. He conceived his master plan while he was in jail in Oporto, Portugal, for embezzling the funds of a company he had taken over. Some criminals sit in jail and try to avoid repeating their misfortunes. Others, like Reis or Tony de Angelis, think up bigger, more foolproof schemes. While he was sitting in his cell, Reis put together his master plan that, if it succeeded, would have made him the richest, and possibly the most influential man in Portugal in only one year.

Unless you have actually tried it, counterfeiting is a very complex operation. To be successful, (i.e., not get caught), be able to spend your money, and not receive free room and board from the government, you have to do three things successfully. First, you have to create counterfeit currency that can't be detected. Second, you need a way of laundering the money and converting it into real assets so you can enjoy the fruits of your ill-begotten labor. Third, you must make sure that you avoid the triple curse of detection, arrest and conviction. Let's see what Reis's solution was to this age-old problem.

Step One: Create an Undetectable Banknote

During the 1920s, the Banco do Portugal had the exclusive right to print currency in Portugal. The bank used foreign printing companies with superior anti-counterfeiting technology to protect their banknotes. The English company, Waterlow & Sons, printed the 500 and 1,000 escudo notes (equal to about $25 and

$50 in 1923) for the Banco do Portugal. So to solve the first problem, Reis asked why not get Waterlow & Sons to print the notes for him?

Reis was a natural-born forger. He forged his diploma as an engineer from Oxford as a "joke." This helped him land a job as a government railroad inspector in Angola at the age of twenty-two. In 1924, he forged $100,000 worth of checks and used the money to take over control of Ambaca, the Royal Trans-African Railway Company of Angola. He then used the money in the company's treasury to cover his own checks. He was arrested in July 1924 for embezzlement, but was released two months later when a court decided his was a civil and not a criminal case.

It was during the two months he was the guest of the Oporto police that he conceived his infamous counterfeiting scheme. The key was to find someone with a respected name who could help him convince Waterlow & Sons to print banknotes secretly for Reis. He found three men of questionable repute, but with connections to help Reis: Jose Bandeira, Gustav Adolf Hennies and Karel Marang.

Bandeira got his brother, the Portuguese Minister to the Netherlands, to give Marang a letter introducing him as a respected Dutch citizen who had a power-of-attorney for Alves Reis to negotiate the printing of the banknotes. Marang went to Waterlow & Sons in London, and presented his letter of introduction as the "Consul General of Persia" on forged Banco do Portugal stationary to Sir William Waterlow.

Marang spun the story Reis had instructed him to give. A private syndicate was being formed to save the colony of Angola from its current dire financial condition with a $5,000,000 investment. In return for the loan, the syndicate would be allowed to print and circulate banknotes in Angola. Waterlow & Sons would print the banknotes for the syndicate, and once the notes reached Angola, the banknotes would be supercharged (overprinted) with the word ANGOLA so they wouldn't be confused with notes from the mother country. The whole affair had to be kept secret lest Angola fall into further financial difficulties due to ill-placed rumors of pending economic ruin.

Of course, Sir William knew that supercharging notes was normal practice for Portugal's colonies, and that the Banco Ultramarino had the exclusive right to print banknotes for the Portuguese colonies. This was an opportunity for Waterlow & Sons to get this business away from Bradbury, Wilkinson & Co., the current printer of banknotes for the Banco Ultramarino in Angola.

Marang asked Waterlow to print the 500 escudo note with Vasco da Gama on it (Figure 5.1). The deal was signed on January 6, 1925, and for the printing cost of $7,200, Reis and his conspirators received $5,000,000 in banknotes, a 70,000 percent return on their investment. Bandeira picked up the first group of notes from Waterlow & Sons on February 10, and by March 20, they had 100 million escudos ($5,000,000) in Portuguese banknotes. Bandeira used his orange diplomatic card to transport the bills in luggage marked the "Legation of Portugal" across the borders without detection. After the first step had been

Figure 5.1 Portugal 500 Escudo Note.

successfully completed, they placed an order for an additional 190 million escudos in banknotes ($9,500,000). Of course, the banknotes never made it to Angola.

Every banknote has a serial number, and in order for the plot to succeed, Reis had to have Waterlow & Sons use the same serial numbers. One risk in the scheme was having banknotes with duplicate numbers discovered, but this was the lesser of two evils. If Reis and Marang had requested banknotes outside the numerical range of the 500 escudo notes, the spurious notes would have been quickly discovered. The lower risk lay in duplicating the existing serial numbers, and hoping the counterfeiters were able to successfully release all the banknotes before the law of large numbers caught up with them.

Step Two: Laundering Money with Your Own Bank

Step One of the plan was complete, now for Step Two: laundering the money. A small-scale counterfeiter can pass bills through petty criminals, but the notes Reis and friends had were equal to almost 1 percent of Portugal's GDP. This was the equivalent of over $150 billion if the same amount had been released in the United States today. Even if Reis had hired every petty criminal in Lisbon and Oporto, he wouldn't be able to unload a fraction of the banknotes he had.

Reis was going first class with his counterfeiting scheme, and he decided the only way to launder the money was to have his own bank. Reis used his newly printed banknotes to encourage corrupt Portuguese officials and politicians to grant him his bank charter, and on June 15, 1925, the Banco Angola e Metropole's application was approved by the government. Reis now owned his own bank. Of course, the bank established multiple branches in Lisbon and Oporto to speed up the distribution of their treasure.

Want to exchange foreign currency? The Banco Angola e Metropole provided the best rates in the country. Want to borrow money for a business or mortgage? The Banco Angola e Metropole was happy to extend you the loan in cash. Want high interest rates on your deposits? Go to the Banco Angola e Metropole. In the meantime, Reis, his wife and their compatriots spent their money freely, buying jewelry, cars, real estate and sending money abroad.

Reis flooded Portugal with his freshly minted banknotes, and the economy of Portugal was booming. And as Reis would rationalize, how was this any different from what a real government did? Was there really any difference between Keynesianism and counterfeiting?

Step Three: Avoid Detection (For a While)

Step Three and the most important of all was how to avoid detection, arrest and imprisonment. For this, Reis had a brilliant solution. Since the conspirators were counterfeiting Banco do Portugal banknotes, only the Bank could initiate proceedings to prosecute them. But what if—just what if—Reis controlled the outstanding shares in the Banco do Portugal? The bank had already exceeded its statutory banknote limit many times over and the directors of the Banco do Portugal had never been prosecuted for breaking the law, so why should they prosecute Reis? Or as Reis put it in a sentence that could have come from Yogi Berra, "How can they arrest us when they're us and we're them?"

Like most European countries, Portugal had suffered inflation after World War I. Prices had increased 48 percent per annum between 1919 and 1924, and the escudo had depreciated by 87 percent against the pound sterling. Although the Banco do Portugal was only supposed to issue banknotes thrice its capital, it had, in fact, issued banknotes a hundred times its capital. Reis's monetary manipulations were minor by comparison. Figure 5.2 shows the depreciation of the Portuguese escudo against the U.S. dollar after World War I.

Reis began buying up as many shares of the Banco do Portugal as he could, so he could gain a controlling interest in the bank to protect himself. Should his scheme ever be detected, Reis would, quite naturally, refuse to prosecute himself. By November 1925, Reis controlled over 10,000 shares of Banco do Portugal stock. "Just another month" and Reis would have control of the Banco do Portugal. Then he could live in luxury for the rest of his life.

As in all of these cases, whether it be counterfeiting currency, pumping and dumping, forging corporate books, hiding money in offshore accounts, or any of the other financial schemes that crooks are heir to, it was hubris and greed

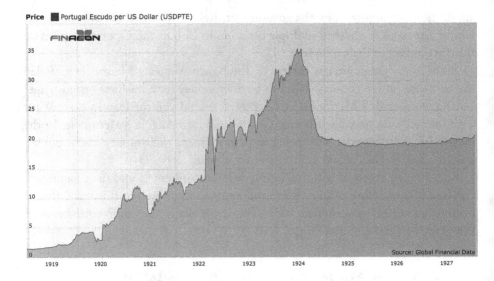

Price ■ Portugal Escudo per US Dollar (USDPTE)

Figure 5.2 Portuguese Escudos per United States Dollar, 1919 to 1927.

which undid Reis. He took part of his proceeds and invested them in a mineral and oil exploitation scheme in Angola hoping to increase his wealth even more. In December 1925, Reis and Hennies were on their way back to Portugal from Angola. Aboard the ship, they learned that the Banco do Portugal was doing an investigation of the 500 escudo notes.

A lowly, underpaid teller who worked part-time as a jeweler to help make ends meet had become suspicious of the Banco Angola e Metropole. The escudo notes he received were never in numerical order (Reis's plan to shuffle the banknotes to avoid detection actually caused detection), and the pages that recorded foreign exchange transactions at the bank were torn out. The teller alerted the Banco do Potugal, an investigation began, and soon duplicate banknotes were discovered.

Hennies, sensing that the scheme was up, decided to sail on, but Reis disembarked in Lisbon. His goal was to lay the blame for the duplicate banknotes on officials at the Banco do Portugal by forging documents that the Governor of the Banco do Portugal was the originator of the whole plot.

The Scam Exposed

The crisis broke on December 4, 1925 when the newspaper *O Sêculo* published an expose of the Banco Angola e Metropole. When one of its branches was closed, huge caches of duplicate 500 escudo banknotes were discovered. Reis, his compatriots, and almost anyone associated with the Banco Angola e Metropole (save Hennies, who had sailed on) were arrested. Incredibly enough, the governor and the vice governor of the Banco do Portugal were also arrested, so convincing were Reis's forged documents. It was as if Ben Bernanke and Janet Yellen had been arrested for counterfeiting!

The Banco do Portugal faced a tough decision. What should it do with all the 500 escudo notes? It was impossible to differentiate between the original and the duplicate banknotes because they were printed by the same printer using the same plates. The Banco do Portugal came to the only conclusion possible. Every single Vasco da Gama 500 escudo note would have to be withdrawn from circulation. People could exchange up to 200 of the Vasco da Gamas for 1,000 escudo notes until December 26. After that, they would be worthless.

The revelation of the counterfeiting plot created a huge loss of confidence in Portugal's corrupt democratic government. Military officers who were aggrieved over their pay failing to keep up with inflation, overthrew the democratic government on May 28, 1926. This eventually led to the dictatorship of Portugal by Dr. Antonio de Oliveira Salazar (who had been Portugal's finance minister) in 1932. Salazar remained dictator of Portugal until his death in 1968. A scheme to counterfeit currency and make a forger rich had led, indirectly, to the downfall of a democracy, which was followed by a forty-year dictatorship.

Reis remained in jail and was found guilty on June 29, 1930 of falsely introducing 330,000 banknotes into Portugal. He was sentenced to twenty years in prison. His compatriots were found guilty as well, but received lesser sentences. Reis was released from prison on May 14, 1945, and died ten years later.

Sir William Waterlow was sued by the Banco do Portugal for damages for printing the banknotes. Of course, Waterlow had no knowledge of the counterfeiting scheme and as his lawyers argued, no actual damage had been done to the bank by the banknotes. If anything, Portugal was better off as a result of Reis's unconventional stimulus plan. Though Waterlow spent a million dollars on lawyers defending him, he lost the case and Waterlow & Sons was forced to pay £610,392 (about $3,000,000) in damages. There must be a certain irony in the fact that as a result of the lawsuit, the main beneficiary of the scheme to counterfeit the banknotes was the Banco do Portugal itself. Sir William died of peritonitis in 1931, and the case was settled in April 1932.

Reis was the last of the great counterfeiters. His scheme had style and panache, as did he. His story ripped through the papers just as his scam ripped through the economy. This tale should not be forgotten, nor should we forget Reis and the ingenuity that rested behind his schemes. Who knows what the digital counterfeiters of the twenty-first century will dream up?

chapter six

Hungary's Horrendous Hyperinflation

If you were to ask most people which country suffered the worst inflation in history, they would probably answer Germany, since Germany's hyperinflation after World War I is probably the most famous. By 1923 when Germany finally put an end to its hyperinflation, it took 1 trillion old marks to get 1 new Rentenmark. As devastating as the German inflation was, there were three hyperinflations that made the German case pale in comparison: Hungary in 1946, Yugoslavia between 1992 and 1994 and Zimbabwe from 2004 to 2009. Of these three, Hungary's was the worst of them all.

Hungary was no stranger to hyperinflation. The Austro-Hungarian Empire was on the losing side of World War I and was broken up after the war. The new nation of Hungary lacked the proper government structures to collect taxes to cover government expenditures, so it turned to printing money to fill the hole in its budget. Before World War I, there were 5 kronen to the U.S. dollar, but by 1924 there were 70,000 kronen to the U.S. dollar. So Hungary replaced the kronen with the pengö at the rate of 12,500 pengö to the kronen in 1926.

Hungary was spared much of World War II's destruction until 1944 when it became a battleground between Russia and Germany. Half of Hungary's industrial capacity was destroyed and 90 percent was damaged. Transportation was difficult because most of the rail lines and locomotives had been destroyed. What remained was either taken back to Germany by the Nazis or seized as reparations by the Russians.

The Collapse of the Pengö

Prices were already rising in Hungary after the war because production capacity fell due to the destruction of Hungary's industrial capacity during the war. With no tax base to rely upon, the Hungarian government decided to stimulate the economy by printing money. It loaned money to banks at low rates, which then loaned the money to companies. The government hired workers, provided loans to consumers and gave money directly to people. The government literally flooded the country with money to get the economy going again. Money may not have grown on trees, but it certainly flowed off the printing presses.

To see how quickly the money supply rose, consider the fact that the currency in circulation stood at 25 billion pengö in July 1945, rose to 1.646 trillion by January 1946, to 65 quadrillion (million billion) pengö by May 1946 and to 47 septillion (trillion trillion) pengö by July 1946.

How bad was the inflation? Something that cost 379 pengö in September 1945, cost 72,330 pengö by January 1945; 453,886 pengö by February, 1; 872,910 by March; 35,790,276 pengö by April; 11.267 billion pengö by May 31; 862 billion pengö by June 15; 954 trillion pengö by June 30; 3 billion billion pengö by July 7; 11 trillion billion pengö by July 15; and 1 trillion trillion pengö by July 22, 1946. Obviously, the inflation was devastating to the mathematically challenged.

At the height of the inflation, prices were rising at the rate of 150,000 percent *per day.* By then, the government had stopped collecting taxes altogether because even a single day's delay in collecting taxes wiped out the value of the money the government collected.

Before the war, in March 1941, there were 5 pengö to the U.S. dollar; by June 1944, there were 33 pengö to the USD and in August 1945 when the real hyperinflation began, there were already 1,320 pengö to the USD. Then, the pengö collapsed. There were 100,000 pengö to the USD by November 1945, 1.75 million by March 1946, 59 billion by April 1946, 42 million million by May 1946 and 460 trillion trillion by July 1946.

Of course, Hungary had taken some failed measures to reduce the inflation. In December 1945, the government imposed a 75 percent capital levy by making people turn in 400 pengö and receive 100 pengö back with a stamp on the banknotes to indicate they were legal tender. But the central bank didn't stop printing money. The hyperinflation made it even more difficult for the government to collect taxes because between the time the taxes were due and they were collected, inflation wiped out the value of the taxes. The government introduced the adopengö, which supposedly was indexed to consumer prices, but even the indexed adopengö succumbed to the inflation.

People Suffer the Ravages of Hyperinflation

So how did people cope with this onslaught of money? How did the government that printed the money handle so many zeroes? The solution was simple: change the name of the currency. The pengö was replaced by the milpengö (1 million pengö), which in turn was replaced by the bilpengö (1 million million pengö) which was replaced by the inflation-indexed adopengö.

Banknotes of a similar deonomination had the same picture on them, but were a different color. The milliard pengö was lavender; the milliard milpengö was blue;

Figure 6.1 Hungary Milliard Bilpengö—the Highest Denomination Note Ever Issued.

and the milliard bilpengö was green—but except for the color, the notes looked alike. Someone who lived through the hyperinflation said they gave up on looking at the denominations and when someone was at a local shop the cashier would say that their bread cost two blues and a green. The milliard bilpengö (Figure 6.1) is the highest denomination note ever printed since it was equal to a billion trillion pengö. Unfortunately, at the end of the inflation, it was only worth about 12 cents USD.

The forint replaced the pengö on August 1, 1946 at the rate of 400,000 quadrillion pengö to the forint; however, the stabilization worked, and prices remained relatively stable in Hungary into the 1960s. As for all the old pengö, they were thrown away because they were worthless.

Who paid the price of the inflation? First off, workers did. Real wages fell by over 80 percent as a result of the inflation, and though the workers had jobs, they were pushed into poverty by the hyperinflation. Creditors were wiped out. Anyone who was owed money was paid off in worthless inflated currency. But production did recover, and by August 1946, the pengö was replaced by the forint which Hungary still uses today.

So did Hungary's inflation achieve the goal of stimulating production? The hyperinflation did raise Hungary's industrial capacity, got the railroads moving again, and got much of the capital stock replaced. However, workers lost 80 percent of their wages and creditors were wiped out.

Politically, however, Hungary's fate was sealed by the communists, who eventually seized power and turned the Republic of Hungary into the People's Republic of Hungary in 1949 with a new constitution modelled on that of the Soviet Union. Hungary probably would have gone communist even if the hyperinflation had never occurred, but the way the hyperinflation wiped out workers and creditors and made them dependent upon the state paved the way for communism's eventual triumph in Hungary.

chapter seven

Slobodan Milošević and the Collapse of Yugoslavia

In a previous chapter, I documented the worst hyperinflation in history, which was suffered by Hungary in 1946. When Hungary finally converted from the pengö to the forint, it took 400,000 quadrillion (million billion) pengö to get one forint! Yugoslavia failed to beat Hungary's record, but if Yugoslavia failed to win the gold in the Inflation Olympics, it wasn't for lack of trying. You can probably blame one person—Slobodan Milošević—for the collapse not only of the country's currency and economy, but for the country itself.

A Socialist Market Economy

Yugoslavia was an amalgam of different ethnicities when it was formed after World War I, and its original name, the Kingdom of the Serbs, Croats and Slovenes indicated its origins. After World War II, Yugoslavia reconstituted itself after suffering from occupation, and Yugoslavia's dictator, Josip Broz Tito, distanced himself from the Soviet Union in 1948 and sought his own socialist path for Yugoslavia.

The country played a unique role during the Cold War. Yugoslavia was a socialist country that relied upon the market to allocate goods. Some economists looked upon Yugoslavia positively as a country that had found the middle ground between the socialism of the Soviet bloc and the capitalism of the West. Unfortunately, this middle ground worked better in theory than in practice.

War, Sanctions and Hyperinflation

Slobodan Milošević became the president of Serbia on May 8, 1989. Though his goal was to restore Yugoslavia's greatness, he was instrumental in destroying

Yugoslavia. The collapse of the country may have been inevitable after Tito died, but the collapse of the economy and currency were not.

The central bank in Yugoslavia was never independent. In January 1991, Slobodan Milošević ordered the Serbian National Bank to issue $1.4 billion in credit to his friends. After Milošević resigned from power, he was charged with corruption and embezzlement because of this and other actions he took.

In 1992, the United Nations imposed sanctions on what was left of Yugoslavia as a result of the carnage that was occurring in Bosnia and Herzegovina. Consequently, both GDP and fiscal revenue declined while the cost to Milošević of fighting his wars with Yugoslavia's former republics rose. Milošević had already raided the Serbian National Bank for funds, and by this time most of the country's hard currency was gone. The sanctions hit Yugoslavia hard, and its financial resources dried up. Milošević saw only one solution to his political survival: print money.

Inflation was nothing new to Yugoslavia. The country had suffered double-digit inflation in every year save one between 1969 and 1986. Inflation rose further after 1985, moving from 87 percent in 1985 to 162 percent in 1987 and to 2,719 percent in 1989.

When the United Nations imposed sanctions on Yugoslavia in 1992, the country quickly collapsed into hyperinflation. Prices increased 17,200 percent in 1992, and an incredible 3 quadrillion percent in 1993. Inflation was 1,788 percent in December 1993 alone and 4,139 percent in January 1994, though one wonders how the government arrived at such exact figures. The hyperinflation finally ended in March 1994, and by 1995, the annual inflation rate was a more "normal" 122 percent. The highest denomination note issued by Yugoslavia, the 500 billion dinars note is illustrated in Figure 7.1.

Figure 7.1 Yugoslavia 500 Billion Dinara Note.

Economic Collapse

The government tried to contain the inflation through bureaucratic measures, such as imposing price controls, though this only exacerbated the situation because bakers and slaughterhouses stopped producing food rather than produce at a loss. Yugoslavia's gas stations were closed, and gasoline could only be bought from black market entrepreneurs on the side of the road. When the government required firms to file paperwork every time they raised prices to discourage price increases, this measure hastened inflation because firms would raise their prices by more than was needed in order to reduce the amount of paperwork they had to file. Instead of controlling inflation, the government spurred inflation.

In November 1993, the government delayed turning on the heat in government-owned apartment buildings in order to save money, so the buildings' tenants bought inefficient space heaters, which overloaded the electrical system leading to blackouts. Pensioners and other Yugoslavs delayed making payments for government services, knowing that even a few days' delay would wipe out the cost of making any payments. Every measure the government took to bureaucratically stifle inflation caused people to respond in a way that fueled inflation and hastened the collapse of the economy. As inflation got worse, businesses began using Deutsche Mark instead of Yugoslav dinars to avoid losing money from the continual erosion in the value of the dinar.

To keep up with the inflation, Yugoslavia had to continually issue new currencies to get rid of the zeroes that were piling up. On January 1, 1990, a new dinar replaced the old dinar at the rate of 10,000 to 1, in July 1992 another dinar was introduced at the rate of 10 to 1, and in October 1993 a third new dinar was introduced at the rate of 1 million old dinar to 1 new dinar. In January 1994 the 1994 dinar was introduced at the rate of 1 billion 1993 dinar to 1 1994 dinar, which was replaced in turn by the super dinar at the rate of 12,500,000 to 1 in less than a month.

In one year, between December 1992 and December 1993, the effective exchange rate between the Yugoslav dinar and the U.S. dollar went from 900 dinars to the U.S. dollar to 3 billion million million dinars (3 sextillion for anyone who cares) to the USD (Figure 7.2). In February 1994, 1 new super dinar was equivalent to 1.2 octillion (1.2 billion billion billion, i.e., 27 zeroes) dinar from 1989. Not even the math majors could keep up.

Milošević is Kicked Out

Despite destroying the economy, Slobodan Milošević battled on and remained in power for another six years. He resigned from office following the disputed elections of September 24, 2000, and he was arrested on March 31, 2001 on

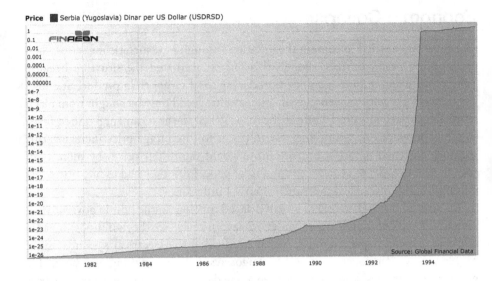

Figure 7.2 Yugoslav Dinars per U.S. Dollar, 1980 to 1995.

suspicion of corruption, abuse of power and embezzlement. The Serbian authorities were unable to prove their case, and Milošević was extradited to the International Criminal Tribunal for the former Yugoslavia in The Hague where he remained until he died in his prison cell on March 11, 2006.

Did Milošević receive a just punishment? Notes issued by colonial Georgia warned that "To counterfeit is death without benefit of clergy." During the French Revolution when *"la loi punit de mort le contrafacteur,"* (the law punishes counterfeiters with death) was printed on their banknotes more people were put to death for counterfeiting than for any other single offense. In England two hundred years ago, counterfeiting was punishable by hanging, not only for counterfeiting currency, but even for passing a counterfeit bill to another person, a law which put a number of innocent people to death.

In his own way, Slobodan Milošević was probably one of the greatest counterfeiters of all time, and though Slobodan Milošević may not have suffered the death penalty for his destruction of Yugoslavia's currency and economy, at least he spent the rest of his life in prison.

chapter eight

The Death and Rebirth of the Zimbabwe Dollar

If Freddy Krueger were a currency, he would be the Zimbabwe dollar. Every time you think he is dead, he comes back to life to destroy the economy.

In 2017, after eight years without a currency of their own, Zimbabwe introduced "Dollar Bond" banknotes. This came only two years after the government announced that they were finally demonetizing the Zimbabwe dollar. Although the U.S. dollar replaced the Zimbabwe dollar in everyday transactions in 2009, banks still carried accounts that were denominated in Zimbabwe dollars. Beginning on June 15, 2015, for only 35 million billion (35,000,000,000,000,000) Zimbabwe dollars, bank customers received one free portrait of George Washington.

Believe it or not, Zimbabwe will not get in the Guinness Book of World Records for the most insane currency conversion of all time. Hungary holds this dubious record because 400,000 quadrillion pengö were required to obtain one forint back in 1946 when Hungary went through its own currency conversion.

In 2015, the United States dollars and South African rand were used in Zimbabwe for everyday transactions. These two currencies were legal tender in Zimbabwe along with Australian dollars, the British pound, the Botswana pula, Chinese yuan, Indian rupees and Japanese yen. Despite the benefits of dollarization, Zimbabwe once again is printing the hated Zimbabwe dollar.

The Zimbabwe Dollar Is Born

Zimbabwe was originally a British colony known as Rhodesia, named after Cecil Rhodes, who obtained a mining concession from a local king. The colony of Rhodesia declared its independence from Great Britain on November 11, 1965, but because it did not allow black citizens any representation in the government, Britain imposed sanctions against Rhodesia. On March 3, 1978, the President of Rhodesia, Ian Smith, signed an agreement to provide black majority rule in Rhodesia. The country was renamed Zimbabwe Rhodesia on June 1, 1979, and Zimbabwe declared its independence on April 17, 1980.

The country's currency was originally the Rhodesia pound which was introduced at par with the British pound sterling. The Rhodesia dollar (RHD) replaced the Rhodesia pound on February 17, 1970 with 2 RHD equal to 1 Rhodesia pound. The Zimbabwe dollar, in turn, replaced the Rhodesia dollar at par on April 18, 1980. When this conversion occurred, a Zimbabwe dollar was valued at 1.47 USD, but because Zimbabwe had higher inflation than the United States, the Zimbabwe dollar steadily depreciated against the U.S. dollar. The Rhodesian dollar was not worth more than a United States dollar for long.

Inflation Explodes

The combination of decreases in farm production following large land redistributions, a decline in the production of goods, a collapse of the banking system, involvement in the Second Congo War in 1998 and a drought in 1999 led to a steady decline in production. Zimbabwe suspended foreign debt repayments in February 2004, resulting in compulsory suspension from the IMF. This, combined with sanctions imposed by the United States, the IMF and the European Union, led to large budget deficits, which could only be covered by printing money, eventually leading to hyperinflation.

The inflation rate in Zimbabwe averaged around 10 percent in the 1980s, around 20 percent to 30 percent between 1990 and 1997, and 50 percent between 1998 and 2000. In 2001, the inflation rate exceeded 100 percent, and in 2003 it was almost 600 percent. At that point, hyperinflation kicked in. Inflation rose to 1,281 percent in 2006, and 66,000 percent in 2007. In 2008, the money supply grew by 658 billion percent and inflation hit an annualized 80 billion trillion percent (89,700,000,000,000,000,000,000) toward the end of 2008. At that point, Zimbabwe dollars were about as valuable as toilet paper, but not as useful.

It's a Miserable Life

The main cause of Zimbabwe's inflation was the excessive money growth of the Zimbabwe dollar, but officials tried to place the blame elsewhere. In 2007, for example, Zimbabwe declared inflation illegal (!), outlawing price increases on some commodities. The government even arrested some corporate executives for increasing prices on commodities, but failed to arrest any of its own officials who were the primary cause of the hyperinflation.

Other problems occurred. People found it difficult to take money out of ATM machines because the ATMs couldn't handle values in billions and trillions. Customers received a "data overflow error" and weren't able to withdraw anything. By the time the ATM machines were fixed and the ATMs allowed customers to withdraw Z$100 billion per day, that amount wasn't enough to cover the cost of a

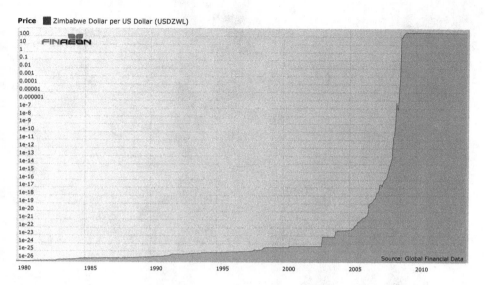

Figure 8.1 Zimbabwe Dollars per United States Dollar, 1960 to 2014.

loaf of bread. If a customer wrote a check to purchase an item, they were required to write the check for twice the cash price of the item to cover the impact of inflation by the time the check cleared.

During the 2000s, Zimbabwe went through four currencies in four years. On July 31, 2006, Zimbabwe introduced a new dollar with 1,000 old Zimbabwe dollars (ZWD) equal to 1 second Zimbabwe dollar (ZWN). On August 1, 2008, 10 zeroes were removed with 1 third Zimbabwe dollar (ZWR) equal to 10 billion second Zimbabwe dollars. On February 2, 2009, a fourth Zimbabwe dollar (ZWL) was introduced, removing 12 zeroes, with 1 fourth Zimbabwe dollar equal to 1 trillion third Zimbabwe dollars. Thus 1 fourth Zimbabwe dollar was equal to 10 trillion trillion (10,000,000,000,000,000,000,000,000 with 25 zeroes) first Zimbabwe dollars. Naturally, the value of the Zimbabwe dollar collapsed relative to the United States dollar as is illustrated in Figure 8.1.

Dollar One, Dollar Two, Dollar Three, Dollar Four

The hyperinflation produced a dazzling array of currency denominations. The highest denomination for the first Zimbabwe dollar was 100,000 dollars. When the first Zimbabwe dollar was converted into the second Zimbabwe dollar at 1,000 to 1, paper currency equal to 1 Zimbabwe cent was printed so old 10 Zimbabwe dollar notes could be converted. Within a year, the Reserve Bank of Zimbabwe was printing a 100 billion dollar note. In total, 32 different denominations of the Zimbabwe dollar were printed within one year.

Figure 8.2 Zimbabwe 100 Trillion Dollar Note.

The third Zimbabwe dollar went through 27 denominations ranging from 1 dollar to 100 trillion dollars. Coins issued under the first Zimbabwe dollar were made legal tender under the third Zimbabwe dollar, increasing their value 10 trillion fold. The machines used to print currency were used continuously, causing them to break down, and creating greater shortages of currency, especially since the Reserve Bank was unable to obtain repair parts for the machines because of the shortage of foreign currency.

The 100 trillion dollar note (see Figure 8.2) was the highest denomination issued for the third Zimbabwe dollar. It has become a novelty item which can be obtained from dealers on eBay. Although its face value is less than one penny, the banknotes generally sell for around $60.

The fourth Zimbabwe dollar died a quick death, only reaching the Z$500 denomination before the currency was cast aside. Foreign currency was effectively legalized as a de facto currency on September 13, 2008, and on January 1, 2009, the Reserve Bank of Zimbabwe allowed U.S. dollars to circulate freely throughout the country. The Fourth Zimbabwe dollar remained legal tender until June 30, 2009 by which time it had lost 95 percent of its value in the five months of its existence. By then, transactions were almost exclusively in U.S. dollars, the Zimbabwe dollar having been abandoned.

Clever Financial Calculations

With inflation galloping ahead on a daily basis, and the Reserve Bank of Zimbabwe updating exchange rates infrequently to hide its rapid depreciation, it was difficult to know how little the Zimbabwe dollar was really worth. With no official figure available, some banks figured out a clever way of calculating the exchange rate by using the Old Mutual Implied Rate (OMIR). Shares of the Old Mutual insurance company traded on both the Harare (Zimbabwe) Stock Exchange and on the London Stock Exchange. By comparing the Zimbabwe dollar price of Old Mutual Stock on the Harare Stock Exchange with the British pound price of Old Mutual Stock on the London Stock Exchange, an implied exchange rate was calculated, which was used to carry out transactions.

Zimbabwe's Zombie Dollar

Since 2009, Zimbabwe has had no currency of its own. It has had to rely upon paper currency imported from other countries to act as a medium of exchange. Since foreign currency is scarce, the economy has suffered from deflation rather than hyperinflation. Another problem Zimbabwe has faced since 2009 is that the country has no locally minted coins to carry out everyday transactions. Stores improvised by using pieces of candy to make change rather than using coins. In 2015, the Reserve Bank of Zimbabwe tried to alleviate the coin shortage by putting new "bond" coins into circulation; however, as one person put it, consumers were distrustful of any coins that didn't have an American president on them.

Today, the USD is the primary medium of exchange in Zimbabwe and inflation has been defeated. Prices declined in Zimbabwe by 0.8 percent in 2014 after rising 0.3 percent in 2013. Zimbabwe has gone from being the king of hyperinflation to having a lower inflation rate than the United States! People in Zimbabwe have lost all trust in the government's ability to control inflation. Other countries that dollarized as a result of inflation, such as Ecuador, remain dollarized years after the U.S. dollar was introduced.

But like Freddy Krueger, the Zimbabwe dollar refuses to die and will haunt the dreams of Zimbabweans before destroying the economy. In 2017, both 2 and a 5 Zimbabwe dollar bond notes were introduced, with 10, 20 and 50 dollar bond notes scheduled to be introduced.

Who knows what path of destruction these banknotes will wreak on the Zimbabwe economy in the next few years? We can only hope that the dollar bond notes die a quick death and for once are not reborn.

chapter nine

The Currency Reform that Created Two Countries

One question I often receive about the German stock and bond indices is why they had a 90 percent decline in June 1948 (Figure 9.2). At first, people think there is an error in the data, but German shareholders actually did lose 90 percent of their capital in one day as a result of the currency reform of June 20, 1948 when Reichsmark were converted into Deutsche Mark.

Despite the loss, the reform ultimately benefitted shareholders, who were unable to sell their stocks at the fixed prices the Nazis had imposed during the war. Although the 1948 currency reform imposed an immediate loss on all shareholders and bondholders, the Reform helped West Germany to emerge from the economic collapse of World War II and begin the *Wirtschaftswunder* (Economic Miracle) that enabled Germany to enjoy decades of solid economic growth and become one of the largest economies on the planet.

Nazinomics

During the 1940s, the German government organized its economy with one goal in mind: to win the war. As in the United States, the government made sure that all goods essential to the war were acquired by the government at a reduced cost. The prices of consumer goods were controlled in order to limit inflation, but the inevitable result was a black market in scarce consumer goods.

Not only were price controls imposed upon goods, but price floors were introduced for stocks and bonds, preventing securities from declining in value. A bombed-out factory isn't worth as much as a fully functioning factory, and industry was run to aid the war effort, not to make profits. If markets had been left to themselves, stock prices would have declined as the tide of the war turned against the Nazis, but the government put a price floor on shares. Since prices didn't reflect the value of the shares, stock markets froze and trading dwindled until it was almost non-existent.

Price floors had been introduced during World War I by the stock markets in London, New York, Berlin and elsewhere for good reason. Although stocks traded at their full price, market makers only had to put up a fraction of the cost of stocks, waiting until settlement day to balance their accounts. A steep decline in prices would have bankrupted many of the stock market's traders, so the price floors were introduced to prevent panic selling.

As a result of the price floors, trading in many securities stopped since no one was willing to buy shares for less than they were worth. Consequently, between January 1943 and June 1948 there was virtually no change in the German stock market index. The German government remained in default on its own foreign currency bonds until 1953, introduced multiple exchange rates, and the government imposed capital controls to stem the flow of money out of Nazi Germany.

The War Ends and the Economy Collapses

After the war ended in Germany, peace prevailed, but the economic situation worsened. The money supply had expanded five-fold between 1939 and 1945, but the prices of many goods were fixed. Although ration coupons were used to allocate some goods, the amounts rationed were insufficient to meet daily needs, and consumers were forced to turn to black markets.

After the war ended, the occupying powers replaced the Reichsmark and Rentenmark with a Military Mark (Figure 9.1). Although the western Allies tried to limit the issue of Military Marks to control inflation, the Soviets were more than willing to print extra marks to pay for the rising costs of occupation. For political, rather than for economic reasons, the western Allies gave copies of the plates for the Military Mark to the Soviets, who began printing excessive amounts of the notes generating inflation. Having suffered from economic collapse and hyperinflation

Figure 9.1 20 Allied Military Marks.

after World War I, Germany was facing a second collapse that might have been worse than the hyperinflationary death spiral of the 1920s.

By the spring of 1948, the German economy was collapsing. Food production was half what it had been in 1938 and industrial production was one-third of its pre-war level. With salaries controlled by the government, wages were low, and many workers failed to show up to work, contributing to the decline in production. Instead, people devoted their time to finding the food they needed to survive. By 1948, anywhere from one-third to one-half of all transactions were on the black market or through barter.

American cigarettes were used as a more reliable currency than paper money since cigarettes held their value. Many soldiers sold their cigarettes on the black market to add to the meager salary they were receiving. Food was so scarce that on weekends, many Germans left the cities for the countryside to try and buy food directly from farmers as the shelves of stores in the city were bare. Some Germans grew food in their backyards to keep from starving.

The Free Market Returns

With the growing tension between the western Allies and the Soviet Union, the need to revive the German economy superseded the need to pacify Germany. The reform of the German currency and economy was overseen by Ludwig Erhard who wanted to replace the government-controlled Nazi economy with one based upon the market. Erhard had refused to support the idea of a centralized economy under Hitler, and his anti-Nazi credentials helped him to secure the support of the Allies over other German economists who wanted to maintain the government controls and rationing, which clearly were impoverishing the nation. Erhard advocated the ending of price controls and a currency reform which would replace the Military Mark with a new currency with a limited money supply called the Deutsche Mark.

By eliminating the Military Mark and replacing it with a smaller supply of Deutsche Mark while simultaneously eliminating all price controls, Erhard hoped to end both inflation and the shortages that plagued the economy. The Deutsche Mark banknotes were secretly printed in the United States and put in boxes that were innocuously labelled "doorknobs" so they wouldn't arouse suspicion. Meanwhile, factories were instructed to withhold the distribution of their goods until the currency reform was introduced so the flood of goods into stores would help the economy to revive as quickly as possible.

On June 20, 1948, the currency reform was introduced. Germans, who had gone to bureaucratic offices to pick up their ration coupons, instead received 40 Deutsche Mark in the new currency and an additional 20 Deutsche Mark soon after. Germans were allowed to exchange a limited amount of their Military Marks

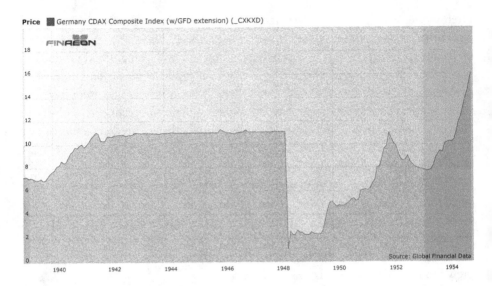

Price ▇ Germany CDAX Composite Index (w/GFD extension) (_CXKXD)

Figure 9.2 Germany Stock Market Index, 1939 to 1954.

into Deutsche Mark, but most of their money was lost. Now goods would be rationed by Deutsche Mark, not by ration coupons.

Stocks and bonds were converted from Reichsmark into Deutsche Mark at the rate of 1 to 10. A bond or stock that had been worth 100 Reichsmark was now worth 10 Deutsche Mark. In effect, the government imposed a 90 percent loss on all securities. This is why GFD's German stock and bond indices (Figure 9.2) show a 90 percent drop in 1948.

Though investors suffered losses, consumers were ecstatic. The effect of the currency reform was immediate. Within a week, store shelves were full, black markets were eliminated, and economic stability returned to Germany. The politics, however, were not so simple.

Germany Becomes a Divided Country

The United States and Britain had not informed the Soviet Union of their plans to reform the German economy and introduce a currency reform. The Reichsmark and Military Mark became worthless overnight in the Bizone (areas controlled by the U.S. and the U.K.), so the old marks began to flood into the Soviet Zone. This forced the Soviets' hand, and a couple of days later, the Soviets introduced their own currency reform, first adding a stamp to currency to validate it, and several months later, introducing new banknotes into circulation.

The Ostmark was introduced in East Germany and continued to circulate there for the next forty years. Although the official exchange rate between the Ostmark

Figure 9.3 100 East German Marks.

(Figure 9.3) and Deutsche Mark was set at one-to-one, the Ostmark always traded at a discount.

I remember when I visited East Berlin in 1986, the black market rate was 5 Ostmark to the Deutsche Mark, but visitors to East Berlin had to exchange 25 Deutsche Mark for 25 Ostmark (which looked like monopoly money) as the price of entering East Berlin to see the walls of Babylon at the Pergamum Museum. The Ostmarks had to be spent in East Berlin, and since I was thirsty, I bought a glass of Vita Cola, the East German version of Coca-Cola, a drink which made cod liver oil taste delicious by comparison. Vita Cola kept the formula for their soft drink secret, but more likely to protect the rest of the world rather than to hide trade secrets.

The currency reform only applied to the three zones occupied by the United States, Britain and France, but not West Berlin. The Soviets followed the currency reform with a blockade of all roads into the Soviet zone making West Berlin inaccessible. The currency reform of June 1948 led directly to the Berlin Blockade and the airlift that saved the people of West Berlin from starvation. Along with the airlift came the Deutsche Mark which became the official currency in West Berlin. After June 1948, the economic and political separation of Germany became a reality and continued until the fall of the Berlin Wall in 1989.

The currency reform was a success. As the economy recovered, the stock market quickly rose in value as well. The German stock index recovered its pre-currency reform level by 1952. On February 27, 1953, Germany officially defaulted on its foreign debts, replacing old bonds with new ones which had a lower interest rate and an extended maturity. Capital controls were soon lifted and the Deutsche Mark became a strong currency that enabled Germany to recover.

Of course, stocks were never allowed to trade in East Germany. Its citizens would have been happy to temporarily lose 90 percent of the value of their investments and see their capital eventually be returned in whole. Instead, East Germans lost everything, and had to wait forty years before the Ostmark was replaced by the Deutsche Mark.

part three

The Insanity of Interest Rates

chapter ten

Greek Loans and Greek Defaults: Déjà Vu All Over Again

In 2012, Greece had the largest sovereign debt default in history. Greece ran budget deficits of 10 percent of GDP in 2008, 15 percent in 2009, 11 percent in 2010 and 10 percent in 2011. Greek government debt, as a share of GDP, rose from 109 percent in 2008 to 180 percent in 2015. At the same time, the Greek economy shrank every year from 2009 to 2013.

Greece received a €110 billion bailout on May 2, 2010, but that proved insufficient, and in February 2012, Greece received an additional €240 billion loan. Private creditors were required to sign a deal extending maturities, lowering interest rates and taking a 53.5 percent loss on the value of the bonds.

Had bondholders studied history, they might have made a different choice before buying Greek bonds. Greece defaulted or restructured its debt in 1826, 1843, 1860, 1893 and 1932. It would be interesting to compare the most recent defaults with what happened to Greek bondholders in the past.

The Greek Loans of 1824 and 1825

Greece issued its first bonds in the midst of its War for Independence, before it was even a country. The Greek rebellion began on March 17, 1821, and was suppressed by the Ottoman Empire in 1825. Russia, the United Kingdom and France came to the aid Greece in 1827, which led to military success in 1828 and independence in May 1832.

On February 21, 1824, Greece issued £800,000 in 5 percent bonds with a par value of £100 at £59 in London and on February 15, 1825, Greece issued £2,000,000 in bonds at £56.50 in London. The riskiness of the bonds was obvious since at their issue, the 1825 bond was already yielding 8.85 percent. The price of the bonds (Figure 10.1) followed the fortunes of independence, and as the Ottoman Empire successfully suppressed the Greek revolt, the prices of the bonds quickly fell. Figure 10.1 looks more like a rollercoaster than the chart of a boring bond.

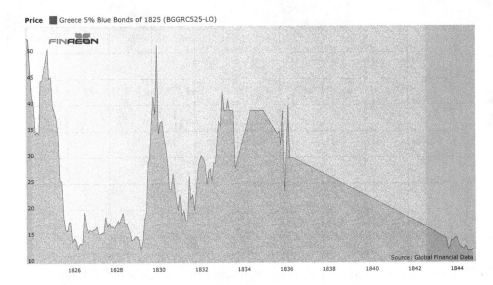

Figure 10.1 Greece 5 Percent Blue Bond Loan of 1825 Price, 1824 to 1844.

The 1824 bonds paid five coupons through July 1, 1826 and the 1825 bonds paid 4 coupons through January 1, 1827. When Greece formally defaulted on the bonds in July 1827, the price dropped to £10.50, a fall of 82 percent from the original issue price in 1825. The price of Greek bonds rose to £54 in April 1830, but quickly fell when it became obvious the newly independent Greece could not honor its debts.

Greece remained in default on these bonds until 1878. As part of one restructuring in 1846, the Greeks detached the coupons due between 1827 and 1846, amounting to £95, from the original bonds and the detached coupons traded separately from the original bonds. By the time the Greeks finally restructured their defaulted debt in October 1878, the 1824 bonds were £275 behind in principal (£100) and interest and the 1825 bonds were £265 behind in principal (£100) and interest. The holders of the 1824 loan received £31 12s for every £100 nominal of the old bonds, the 1825 bondholders at the rate of £30 10s for every £100, and the holders of detached coupons £11 12s for every £100.

The Greek Loan of 1833

The most interesting part of this saga is that Greece was able to issue new bonds while the country was in default. After Greece gained its independence, Otto of Bavaria was placed on the throne of Greece by England, France and Russia. The three Allied Powers agreed to guarantee a £2,100,000 loan for Greece, of which £550,000 went to the Ottoman Empire for territory it ceded to Greece. Holders of the 1824 and 1825 debt voiced their complaints about their subordination to the new bondholders to Lord Palmerston, the British secretary of state for foreign affairs, but to no avail.

Greece issued £2,343,750 in bonds that were jointly guaranteed by England, France and Russia, with each country guaranteeing £781,250 of the loan. The bonds traded separately from each other outside the London Stock Exchange since Greece was still in default. All the revenues of Greece were hypothecated as security for the payment of the loans, and a sinking fund was established, but Greece discharged only a very small portion of the loan.

The interest and principal were paid by the three Allied powers since Greece defaulted until the loans were all discharged by 1871. This cost to the three Allied governments of this guarantee was £3,222,671 in principal and interest which Greece never paid. The European governments that offer to guarantee Greece's current loans might think twice given their experiences of the nineteenth century.

Having settled their outstanding loans in 1878, Greece obtained loans from bankers in London and Paris in 1879 and was able to issue a new 5 percent bond in London in 1881, only to default on this and other newly issued bonds in 1893. Another default occurred in 1932.

It should be remembered that Greece was not the only European country to default on its loans in the nineteenth and twentieth centuries. Defaults and restructurings occurred for many European countries, including

- Austria in 1868, 1914 and 1932,
- Bulgaria in 1915 and 1932,
- Germany in 1932,
- Hungary in 1931
- Italy in 1940,
- Poland in 1936 and 1981,
- Portugal in 1834 and 1892,
- Romania in 1915, 1933 and 1981,
- Russia in 1917 and 1998,
- Serbia/Yugoslavia in 1895, 1933 and 1983,
- Spain in 1831, 1867 and 1882, and
- Turkey in 1876, 1915, 1940 and 1978.

Conclusion

Markets work the same today as they did in the 1820s—when bondholders foresee default, bond prices fall. At the same time, politics work in the twenty-first century just as they did in the nineteenth century. In the case of sovereign debt, politics is more important than finance. Russia, England and France paid a heavy price in guaranteeing the Greek loan of 1833, and European governments ended up paying that price again.

Will Greece default again? Who will pay for it then? Today, the European Central Bank and the IMF bear the cost of Greek defaults but will they write a blank check forever? At some point, even these international agencies will say "NO."

chapter eleven

Seven Centuries of Government Bond Yields

Global Financial Data has put together an index of government bond yields stretching back seven centuries. This index, illustrated in Figure 11.1 uses government bonds from the leading economic powers of each century to measure the long-term changes in government bond yields.

The Changing Center of Financial Power

Over the past eight centuries, the locus of economic power has gradually shifted from Italy to the Netherlands to Great Britain and to the United States. The country at the center of the world's power and economy issues bonds to the rest of the world to cover expenses. Investors in that country and abroad purchase the bonds they issue because they represent the safest bonds that are available for investment.

The country at the locus of economic power can issue more bonds at a lower cost because of the lower risk of being the financial center of the world. Over time, power ebbs away from that country and investors begin placing their money in the bonds of the new world economic power.

Italy was the center of the western economic world until the 1500s. At that time, the Mediterranean was the gateway to Byzantium, the Middle East, and through those countries, to India and China. The Italian city-states of Venice, Genoa, Florence and others grew from this trade, but also fought wars against each other requiring funds for their expenses. After 1500, trade began to shift to the Atlantic ocean.

By the 1600s, the nexus of economic power had shifted to the Netherlands as trade in the Atlantic and with northern Europe enabled the Dutch to strengthen their role in the global economy. The surplus of capital in the Netherlands is illustrated by the fact that the Tulipmania, the world's first financial bubble, occurred in the Netherlands in the 1630s.

The Netherlands was too small to maintain its role as the center of the global economy for long, and the combination of trade, the commercial revolution and the industrial revolution moved the center of economic power to Great Britain at the end of the 1600s. The Glorious Revolution of 1688 realigned political power in England and put Britain on a sound economic footing that would enable it to remain the center of world economic and political power until 1914.

After World War I, the center of economic power shifted from London to New York, and New York remains the center of the global economy today. The dollar is the world's reserve currency, a fact that enables Washington to issue bonds at a lower cost than would otherwise be the case.

Bond Yields Over Time

GFD's Index of Government Bonds uses bonds from each of these centers of economic power to trace the course of interest rates over the past seven centuries. From 1285 to 1600, Italian bonds are used. Data are available for the *Prestiti* of Venice from 1285 to 1303 and from 1408 to 1500, while data from 1304 to 1407 use the Consolidated Bonds of Genoa and the *Juros* of Italy from 1520 to 1598.

General Government Bonds from the Netherlands are used from 1606 to 1699. Yields from Britain are used from 1700 to 1914, using yields on Million Bank stock (which invested in government securities) from 1700 to 1728 and British Consols from 1729 to 1918. From 1919 to date, the yield on United States 10-year bonds is used.

Bond yields are determined by a number of factors. These include 1) the growth in real GDP, 2) the inflation rate, 3) supply and demand factors, and 4) risk.

The yield on a risk-free government bond should equal the growth in nominal GDP since that represents the opportunity cost of holding a government bond both in terms of investment opportunities (real GDP) and the time value of money (inflation). Higher levels of growth or higher inflation will lead to higher interest rates. Increases in the number of bonds (demand for savings) will lead to higher interest rates, while increases in savings will lead to lower interest rates. Finally, the perceived riskiness of the bonds can lead to higher interest rates. Investors may fear that the government may fail to pay back the bonds, reduce the real cost of the bonds through inflation, or depreciate the currency as a way of reducing the cost of repaying the bonds.

The clear trend over the past seven centuries has been for bond yields to decline. This cannot be attributed to lower economic growth or lower inflation, but must clearly be attributed to lower risk of default. Between 1285 and the mid-1600s, yields on government bonds fluctuated between 6 percent and 10 percent and in some cases shot up to 20 percent. Because there is little data on government bond yields before the 1700s, the spikes in yields that occur can be attributed to specific events that affected the issuers, generally the risk of default stemming from wars that occurred. It may very well be that yields on other securities were lower at different points in time up to the 1700s, but the paucity of data makes it difficult to determine this. Nevertheless, the trend is clear.

Since 1700, well-developed markets for bonds have existed in London and New York enabling the yields on government bonds to be traced with accuracy. Since the mid-1600s, the average yield on government bonds has been around 4 percent. Before the 1600s, high interest rates were driven by risk; since the 1600s, high interest rates have been driven by inflation.

Being the center of economic power provides benefits to the issuing country because it can issue bonds at a lower yield than other countries. In the long run, lower interest rates can lead to an overissue of debt if the country chooses to take advantage of its position as the center of the financial world. With the mushrooming U.S. government debt, some people are beginning to wonder whether the United States will be able to continue to maintain its position as the world's central economic power. Before looking at the United States, let's look at government bond yields in Italy, the Netherlands and Britain in the past.

Italian Bond Yields

Because of the paucity of data from before 1700, bond yields as given in Sidney Homer's *A History of Interest Rates* are used. The two principal sources are the *Prestiti* of Venice and the Consolidated Bonds of Genoa.

During medieval times, governments used taxes on trade and revenues from monopolies, on salt for example, to cover expenses, but inevitably wars broke out leading to the need to raise additional money.

Genoa and Venice used "forced loans" as a way of raising funds from its citizens. The two city-states consolidated these forced loans and allowed creditors to sell and trade these forced loans on open markets turning them into modern-day bonds. The debts had no maturity date, but during periods of peace, the government used surplus revenues to retire some of these debts.

Governments that met interest payments on their forced loans, paid off debts during peace times, and did not default on these debts could establish confidence in their debt, enabling them to issue more bonds at a lower yield in the future. As Venice prospered, it increased its ability to service its loans. Venice established a fund to repurchase *prestiti*, floated voluntary loans when necessary, borrowed in anticipation of future tax collections, and established a credible record of repayment. This enabled the cities of Venice and Genoa to borrow money at 6 percent to 10 percent during medieval times and during the Renaissance, rather than the 10 percent to 15 percent that other rulers had to pay.

Dutch Bond Yields

As the center of trade shifted out of the Mediterranean and into the Atlantic after 1500, so shifted economic power. The rulers of Spain, France and England periodically defaulted or forced loans on their subjects, and failed to establish a record of regular repayment that would have enabled them to become the financial centers of Europe.

The Netherlands successfully liberated itself from Spain between 1568 and 1648. The Dutch established the Dutch East India Company in 1602 and the Dutch West India Company in 1621. The Netherlands didn't have to pay for an expensive court, fought their wars at home rather than abroad, profited from international trade, and saved money. The Amsterdam Exchange dealt not only in shares of the Dutch East India Company and Dutch West India Company, but in government bonds as well.

Most securities were in the form of annuities issued by the individual provinces, the United provinces and the towns. This is the essential way in which Dutch lending differed from Italian lending. The Italian credit system relied upon a system of private international banking. The Medicis and other commercial bankers would lend their funds to states, knowing the risks involved. The Italians also had officially chartered banks that intermediated deposits and loans.

Outside of the Italian city-states, loans to heads of state were basically personal loans that clearly ran the risk of default. Spanish, French and English kings borrowed when they had to, defaulted when they couldn't pay, but had no system of drawing upon the savings of the public to guarantee repayment. The Dutch, on the other hand, developed state finance based upon the government's ability to pledge its revenues against the annuities they had issued. Having no royal court, and relying upon local governments, the Dutch paid off loans on time with little risk of default. As risk declined, interest rates fell to 4 percent, the lowest they had ever been in history, and a rate consistent with the low level of default risk that governments enjoy today.

English Government Bond Yields

The Glorious Revolution of 1688 transformed England politically and economically. Unlike his predecessors, William III was a constitutional monarch. Though he had no pretensions to absolute personal power, and though in theory he borrowed on behalf of the English people, he also represented the Whig mercantile interests, which backed him and dominated Parliament. The Bank of England was established in 1694, borrowing at 8 percent (when Dutch rates were at 3–4 percent), and in 1720, the attempt to convert existing government debt into shares in the South Sea Company created the South Sea Bubble. By the 1740s, interest rates had declined to the 3 percent range and in 1751 the 3 percent British Consols were issued to replace existing government debt and annuities.

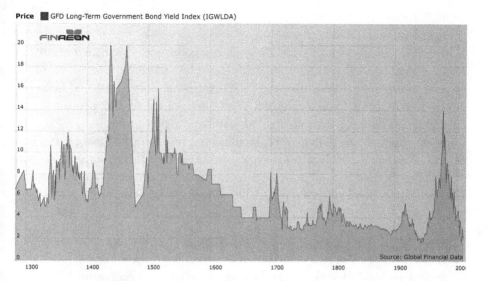

Figure 11.1 GFD's Long-term Government Bond Yield Index, 1285 to 2012.

As can be seen by the graph in Figure 11.1 of long-term interest rates, the risk of default on British debt has been almost non-existent as illustrated by the consistently low interest rates, except in times of inflation. During the Napoleonic Wars, Britain's government debt as a share of GDP exceeded 200 percent, but government bond yields stayed below 6 percent. After 1815, British capital funded canals and railroads in the UK, America and other countries, mines in Latin America, Britain's Colonial bonds and foreign bonds issued by every government in the world. Britain's government debt as a share of GDP shrank to 20 percent of GDP by 1914. Interest rates on government bonds fell below 2.5 percent in 1896, enabling Britain to reduce the interest rate on its Consols to 2.5 percent.

Other countries also benefited from the decline in interest rates. The United States, Germany, France and other countries were all able to issue government debt at 3 percent by the end of the 1800s, whereas at the beginning of the 1800s, 5–6 percent or even more was the norm. Small government, due to few or small wars, combined with shrinking government debt reduced the risk of default and lowered interest rates throughout the world.

United States Bond Yields

World War I shifted the world's financial center from London to New York. In 1915, British bond yields rose above American yields for the first time in history and have remained that way ever since. The United States has never defaulted on its government bonds, so increases in interest rates have been driven mainly by higher rates of economic growth, inflation, and the supply and demand for government bonds.

There are several clear trends in United States government bonds. From 1902 to 1920, 10-year bond yields rose from 2.82 percent to 5.67 percent, with most of the increase occurring between 1914 and 1920 due to the risks of war and inflation. From 1921 to 1945, interest rates fell from 5.67 percent to 1.55 percent due to deflation, depression and the manipulation of bond yields during World War II by the government. From 1945 to 1981, interest rates rose from 1.55 percent to 15.84 percent. This was the highest level for government bond yields in almost 500 years as inflation spiraled out of control due to Keynesian economic policies. Between 1981 and 2016, bond yields fell from 15.85 percent to 1.37 percent.

Bond Yields in the Twenty-First Century

What will Figure 11.1 look like at the end of the twenty-first century? The clear driving factor for bond yields over the past centuries has been the responsibility or irresponsibility of national governments. From Venice and Genoa to the Netherlands, Britain and the United States, when governments kept borrowing to a minimum and paid off their debts, interest rates fell, benefitting not only the national, but the global economy. The 1700s and 1800s had the lowest interest rates in history up until that point in time. The 1900s enjoyed both some of the lowest and the highest interest rates, depending upon the level of inflation generated by the government. Since the risk of default is low, it is inflation and the supply and demand for bonds that has driven interest rates since the mid-1700s.

Government bond yields are now at their lowest level in the past 700 years. In some countries, 10-year bonds now trade at negative interest rates. Whether yields start to rise from here will depend upon the behavior of the government and its willingness to balance its books. Although U.S. government debt has increased to over 100 percent of GDP, this is no guarantee that interest rates will rise. Britain's debt exceeded 200 percent of GDP after the Napoleonic Wars and Japan has run deficits for 20 years with its government debt now over 200 percent of GDP. In both cases, interest rates remained low, and in 2016, Japanese 10-year government bonds had negative yields.

Nevertheless, Britain paid off its debt during the 1800s keeping interest rates from rising. Japan has seen no growth in nominal GDP during the past 20 years, and has been able to rely upon domestic savings and Central Bank intervention to fund its growing government debt. Currently, there is no prospect that the United States will begin to pay off its debt as Britain did in the 1800s, and low interest rates are little consolation if your economy is not growing.

Even if the United States were to suffer the fate of Japan and fail to grow for the next 20 years, which is unlikely, its inability to fund its debt domestically, and the inevitable growth of China, India and other emerging markets, is likely to drive growth and interest rates upward in the decades to come. Although the United States may not default on its debt, it can reduce the burden of its debt through inflation or depreciation. If this were to occur, the balance of financial power could shift again. Whether United States bond yields are used in this graph at the end of the twenty-first century, or those of China, India or some other country will depend upon the fiscal constraint or profligacy of the U.S. government.

Déjà Vu Again and Again: When Moral Hazard Meets a Serial Defaulter

The saga of the European Default continues with Greece playing the starring role. If this were a play, the audience would be shouting at the director "will this show never end?" All kidding aside, the Greek debacle is no small affair and has been making headlines for years. All this is nothing new. Greece has one of the worst track records of any country in Europe when it comes to defaulting on bonds. For sovereign governments that default, there is no "three strikes and you're out."

Between 1826 and 1964, Greece was in default for 90 of those 138 years, so it should come as no surprise that Greece will most likely become the first euro member to default. In the good old days, countries defaulted first and came to an agreement with creditors later. Unfortunately, this is not the case as the European Union acts like a nursemaid trying to protect all its countries or groups from being hurt by a default. So what does the European Union do? They provide a bailout for a protected class and spread the cost on to everyone else.

Greece is a serial defaulter, and the European Union has kept forgiving Greece's transgressions. In economics, this is called moral hazard, which exists when a group can act however it wants because they will not have to take responsibility for their actions.

A Pattern of Serial Defaults

The chapter "Greek Loans and Greek Defaults: Déjà Vu All Over Again" detailed Greece's first default of 1827 when it managed to default even before gaining independence. The three Great Powers (Great Britain, France and Russia) guaranteed a loan of £2,100,000 in 1833 to help Greece after it gained independence. Since Greece was in default on previous loans, the Greek government couldn't issue any new loans, so they had to receive a guarantee for the 1833 loan. As you might guess, Greece defaulted on this loan as well, sticking Great Britain, France and Russia with the bill.

Greece remained in default on its bonds until 1878. As part of one restructuring in 1846, the Greeks detached the coupons due between 1827 and 1846 from the original bonds and they traded separately. By the time the Greeks finally restructured their defaulted debt in October 1878, the 1824 bonds were £275 behind in principal and interest. Bondholders received £31.6 for every £100 nominal of the old bonds, of which £275 was due (an 88.5 percent write down).

Having settled their outstanding loans in 1878, Greece was able to issue a new 5 percent loan to help build the Piraeus-Larissa Railway and issue a monopoly loan. Greece pledged revenues from tobacco taxes, revenues from national lands and plantations and some customs receipts. Despite this, Greece still defaulted in 1893.

After war with Turkey in 1897, a Special Commission was appointed by the Six Great Powers: Great Britain, France, Germany, Austria-Hungary, Italy and Russia, who examined the finances of Greece and put together the Settlement of 1898. Greece threw everything into the debt-guarantee pot, monopolies on salt, petroleum, matches, playing cards, cigarette paper and Naxos Emery; stamp and tobacco dues; and Piraeus customs (import) duties. Interest payments were lowered to 43 percent of the monopoly loan and 32 percent of other loans and a sinking fund of 1 percent per annum of original interest was required to 1902 and 2 percent thereafter.

To make sure Greece paid, the country was put under an International Financial Commission that had the responsibility of collecting the revenues to pay off the debt. After the Commission paid off the portion of the debts due for that year, the remainder was returned to the Greek Government.

Not having the Greeks run Greece worked out pretty well and Greece managed to stay out of default until 1922 when Greece began paying reduced interest on some of its loans from the 1800s. Following a banking crisis in 1931, Greece plunged back into default and Greece reduced the interest payments on all of its debt in July 1932 to 25 percent of interest due and suspended all principal payments. When Greece was occupied by Germany and Italy in April 1941, the country suspended all interest payments. The hyperinflation of 1941 to 1944 wiped out the value of all internal debt and no principal or debt payments were made until 1963.

The Greek government offered to settle its outstanding USD debt on December 31, 1962, reducing its interest payments from 6 to 7 percent to 2.00 to 2.35 percent, rising to 3 percent by 1967. Coupons before 1950 received no interest, and coupons between 1950 and 1962 received 2.00 to 2.35 percent interest. This settlement was applied to all Greek debt in 1964.

The Agreements of 1898 and 1964 didn't require Greece to redeem its debt, but laid down sinking fund requirements for gradually retiring outstanding debt and forgave most outstanding interest payments. Greece had outstanding debt from 1881 that was still outstanding until the 1960s. The concept of 10-year bonds that get rolled over into new 10-year bonds is a relatively new concept that became more popular than sinking fund bonds after World War II.

Out of Default at Last

So how has Greece managed to avoid default since 1964? Simple, they joined the European Union in 1981. Being part of the European Union meant that Greece got a constant influx of money from the rest of Europe to promote development, reducing the need to rely on internal taxes to fund spending and to default when spending exceeded revenues.

But some things never change. Greece joined the Euro in 2001, two years later than the other original members. In order to join, each country had to get its government deficit below 3 percent of GDP and either have government debt below 60 percent of GDP or have its debt shrinking as a share of GDP. After Greece was admitted to the Euro, the Greek government admitted they had cooked the books to get in. Greece suffered no consequences as the leaders of the EU turned a blind eye to this fraudulent behavior. Countries were supposed to keep their government deficit under 3 percent of GDP and when Portugal exceeded this limit, there were threats of imposing financial penalties on Portugal if they didn't change. But when France and Germany exceeded the 3 percent limit, the European Union decided to forgo any financial punishment for any country, paving the way for future Greek excesses. Still, no consequences.

Banks were told they could use the debt of any country as default-free collateral to meet Basel credit requirements, and with Greek bonds paying higher yields than German bonds, the flood gates were opened. No punishment, lots of rewards. Greece lied about its finances again during the Financial Crisis of 2008, and the consequence? Germany led a concerted effort (with 16 countries helping out Greece) to provide a credit transfusion to Greece since they are unable to go to the financial markets.

Default and Move On

German politicians are happy to use German taxpayers' money to bail out Greece, but most German taxpayers, as well as the taxpayers of other countries, are tired of eternally bailing out the Greeks.

Greece is a serial defaulter. Like an outlaw that can't be reformed, Greece kept breaking the rules. When default became inevitable, Germany and the rest of the EU sent Greece hundreds of billions of dollars as Greece could get nothing from the open market. So what incentive does Greece have to change its behavior?

The problem is not just Greece. It is the entire EU political system. The European Union was originally established to create a common market, using a single currency and reducing the boundaries of trade, labor and capital. However, the original reasoning behind the establishment of the European Union has not been maintained. Rather, the political side of the European Union has now taken over and it has now become a massive redistribution machine.

Politics Trumps Economics

Rule number one of economics is politics always trumps economics. Creating a single market in Europe, just as the one in the United States, was a good economic idea provided supporting policies could have been maintained. But when Germany and France allowed Greece to operate outside of proper practices and forgave its indiscretions, this established a pattern of disciplinary negligence. By allowing their banks to buy Greek debt as if it were the same quality as German debt, they only helped to create the conditions they now regret.

Most German taxpayers say, let Greece default. Once the current financial crisis is over with, Greece will start breaking the rules again using the threat of default to get hundreds of billions from the rest of Europe. Greece is like a member of the Mafia who goes over to Germany and says, "Nice little currency you got there, give me a hundred billion or I'll smash it." Avoiding default only drags the crisis out and raises the eventual cost to Europe. It's time to let Greece default and move on.

Birds, Boats and Bonds in Venice: The First AAA Government Bond Issue

When most people think of Venice, they think of the visuals of Venice: the canals, the gondoliers, the paintings by famous artists such as Canaletto or Titian, the Bienniale, or St. Mark's Square (named after the saint whose relics the Venetians stole from Alexandria in 828 by hiding them beneath pork to get them past the Muslim inspectors) and its pestering pigeons.

Birds, Boats and Bonds

When I think of Venice, I think about three things. I think about the first time I went to Europe with my dad. For an entire week before we got to Venice, all I heard about was his insistence on going on a gondola, and passing through the canals while the gondolier sang his Venetian songs. By the time we got to Venice, I was so sick of this that the first thing I did was take him to the canal where you hired gondoliers so I would never have to about the canal ride again. My dad asked our potential gondolier how much the ride was, and when he found out it was the equivalent of $50 (this was a long time ago), he swore at the gondolier and said he wasn't wasting $50 on a stupid boat ride. I was ready to kill my dad, but I didn't cherish the idea of spending the rest of my life in a Venetian prison and having to pass over the Bridge of Sighs.

Since I am an economist, the other two things I think about deal with finance. First, Venice was one of the three city-states in Italy (Florence in 1252, Genoa in 1253, and Venice in 1280) that reintroduced gold into the Italian peninsula eight centuries after the fall of Rome. The other important financial contribution that I associate with Venice are the *prestiti*: the government bonds Venice began issuing in the 1100s to fund its wars. The *prestiti* were the first Eurobonds and if Moody's and S&P had been around in the 1300s, the *prestiti* would have been the first AAA-rated government bonds, though they eventually would have been downgraded.

Prestiti: The First Eurobonds

Venice was the first country to issue government bonds to its citizens in the same way governments currently issue government bonds. Before the Venetian *prestiti*, and even after, kings, queens, emperors and other rulers borrowed money to fight wars or feed their royal megalomania. When the rulers were unable to pay back the loans, they simply defaulted, often bankrupting their creditors.

Venice was different. Venice was the medieval equivalent of Athens, a democracy for the elites. In 726, the Venetians rebelled against their Roman/Byzantine rulers over the Iconoclast controversy and elected the first of 117 doges before Napoleon conquered the city in 1797. Venice became a city-state, expanding its commercial reach, and became an imperial power, eventually capturing and sacking Constantinople in 1204 during the Fourth Crusade. By the late-thirteenth century, Venice was the most prosperous city in all of Europe. At the peak of its power and wealth, Venice had 36,000 sailors operating 3,300 ships, dominating Mediterranean commerce. Defending their empire meant wars with other Italian city-states, such as Florence and Genoa—and wars meant borrowing money.

Price of Prized Perpetuities

Venice introduced the *prestiti* in the twelfth century. Subscriptions were obligatory on wealthy citizens in proportion to their wealth, and the elites of Venice found forced loans preferable to outright taxation. In 1262, Venice lost control over Constantinople, and the outstanding loans, which had been considered temporary, were consolidated into one permanent fund called the *monte vecchio*. This move institutionalized the *prestiti* as long-term loans rather than short-term borrowings. The *prestiti* paid a nominal interest rate of 5 percent on the outstanding capital, two installments of 2.5 percent paid per annum. After 1377, interest rates were variable, and rates were reduced to 4 percent in the 1400s. In 1482 a new series of *prestiti*, the *monte nuovo*, was issued based upon a new kind of tax, and the interest rate was restored to 5 percent. Another new series, the *monte novissimo*, was issued in 1509 during the war with the League of Cabrai, and finally the *monte sussidio* was introduced in 1526.

The *prestiti* were perpetuities that had no specific maturity date. No physical bonds were issued, but all bonds were registered through Venice's loan officers, the *Ufficiali degli Prestiti*. The claims on these bonds could be sold and transferred to others, who then had all the rights of the original purchasers. When possible, the Venetian government repaid the principal. The *prestiti* became popular forms of investment for Venetian nobles. They were also used as endowments for charities, and were used as dowries for daughters upon their marriage.

Unlike in the other kingdoms of Europe, the elites of Venice owned *prestiti* and were part of the government, this reduced the likelihood the city would default on its debts (though the government did forgo interest payments in 1379 to 1381, 1463 to 1479 and 1480). Owning *prestiti* was a privilege. Foreigners, who trusted the Venetian government more than their own, could only obtain *prestiti* through an act of the Council of Venice. The *prestiti* were fully paid off by the government of Venice in the late 1500s.

As with any bond, as the price of the *prestiti* went down, the yield went up. During a war, the price of *prestiti* would fall as new bonds were issued, and owners faced the risk of delays in payment of principal and interest. During peacetime, the price rose as the risk of default diminished. Since the price of trades in *prestiti* was a matter of public record, potential purchasers could use these prices to determine the riskiness of their investment. Thus, the *prestiti* became a barometer of the Venetian Republic's economic health. When there was peace, the government would repay outstanding *prestiti*, sometimes by issuing new *prestiti*, rolling over old loans into new, but when Venice was at war, the government would issue new *prestiti*. The *prestiti* were exempt from tax levies until 1378, from assessment of new forced loans if held by the original owner, and new assessments were levied largely on real estate.

Venice was successful with the issue of *prestiti* because the right to transfer the bonds through the *Ufficiali degli Prestiti* made the bonds liquid and fungible. The Venetian government established a long record of regular payment of interest even when war and disaster threatened the state, assuring investors that they would not lose their money because of a government default. As Venice prospered, confidence in payments rose. The government was under a legal obligation to pay the *prestiti*, and payment was not left to the whim of the king. During peacetime, extra revenues were directed to repayment of the *prestiti*, rather than setting aside money for the Venetian war chest or expanding services. The government had a deliberate policy of repurchasing *prestiti* whenever their price fell. In short, the *prestiti* were the AAA bonds of their day, and as Venice prospered, so did the city and its bondholders.

The Vagaries of War Impact the *Prestiti*

As all nations know, wars do not always go as planned. Sidney Homer, in his *History of Interest Rates*, provides historical data on the prices of *prestiti*, and you can see how the price of the bonds and their yield fluctuate in response to the fortunes of Venice. When Venice imposed large assessments, as in 1311 to 1314, the price of the *prestiti* fell, and when Venice made large repayments, as in 1344, the price could exceed 100. The worst decline in the 14th century came during the War of Chioggia with Genoa between 1378 and 1381, during which Venice imposed very large assessments, suspended interest payments, made the *prestiti* no longer immune from tax levies, and expanded the debt 6 to 9 times its level in 1344. The price sank as low as 19 as a result.

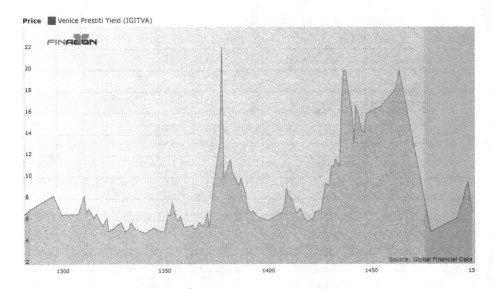

Figure 13.1 Venice *Prestiti* Yield, 1285 to 1500.

After the War of Chioggia ended, the *prestiti* fought their way back as confidence in the Venetian government returned, causing the price to rise to the 60 level. Unfortunately, the fifteenth century was one of ongoing wars in the Mediterranean. Venetian wars with Hungary in 1412, the Turks in 1416, Milan during the 1420s, and wars with both Florence and Milan in 1450 and the costs associated with these wars reduced confidence in the Venetian government's ability to fund the *prestiti*. Emboldened by the fall of Constantinople in 1453, Sultan Mehmet II declared war on Venice, leading to a disastrous and protracted conflict between 1464 and 1479 which drove the price of *prestiti* back to the 20s. This led to the reissue of new *prestiti* as *monte nuova* in 1482.

Figure 13.1 shows the yield on the *prestiti* from 1285 to 1502, assuming a 5 percent coupon (though in reality the *prestiti* paid a variable rate after 1377 and 4 percent during part of the 1400s). The impact of the War of the Chioggia in the 1370s and the wars with Milan and the Turks after 1420 are clearly seen. As the Venetian Republic's empire shrank, holders of the *prestiti* suffered. Venetian bonds would definitely have been downgraded as the heavy impact of the Venetian wars had their effect on the city-state's finances.

Venice never recovered from the devastating war with the Turks, not only because of the loss of its colonies in the Mediterranean, but because Portugal's discovery of a sea route to India and Christopher Columbus's discovery of America shifted the locus of economic power from the Mediterranean to the Atlantic. The ocean-faring sailing ships of France, England and the Dutch Republic replaced Venice's oared galleys. Amsterdam replaced Venice as the financial center of Europe, and during the 1600s and 1700s the East India Company dominated the oceans around Asia the way Venice had dominated the Mediterranean until then. On May 12, 1797, Napoleon Bonaparte brought an end to the Venetian Republic when he conquered the city.

Though Venice is no longer a city-state, it has left us a beautiful city which tourists cherish. It also leaves us an important financial legacy: a record of the first international government bonds which were used throughout Medieval Europe by investors who wanted a safe place to store their wealth. Today, U.S. government bonds play the same role in the twenty-first century that *prestiti* played in the fourteenth century. Let's hope U.S. government bonds can continue to play that role for the centuries to come.

chapter fourteen

German Interest Rate Yields Hit An All-Time Low—Maybe Not

The yield on German 10-year bonds became negative, hitting –0.20 percent on July 6, 2016. This means it would take 1,002 euros in 2016 to get back 1,000 euros in 2017, or 1,020 euros in 2016 to get back 1,000 euros in 2026. The only OECD countries with lower interest rates are Japan and Switzerland. There is virtually no risk Germany will default, so getting almost all of your money back is better than not getting it back at all.

Although these yields appear to be the lowest in history, they actually are not. Germany defaulted twice on its obligations during the twentieth century, impoverishing investors in its bonds. With no prospect of default on the horizon, investors are not as bad off as the owners of German bonds were in the twentieth century.

The first German default occurred as a result of the hyperinflation that Germany suffered during the 1920s. What was interesting about the impact of the hyperinflation on government bonds is that the bonds rose in price in line with inflation even though the interest payments did not. In October 1923, the 3 percent consolidated government bond traded at 37 million marks. This was quite a high price for a bond paying only 3 marks in interest. In effect, the bond was yielding less than 0.00001 percent.

Why, you might ask, would someone pay 37 million marks for a bond that pays 3 marks in interest? The answer is easy: speculators were hoping that once the inflation was over, the government would redeem the bonds at their inflation adjusted value. Speculators buying the 3 percent perpetuities of Germany thought the government would revalue the bonds, providing them with both a hedge against hyperinflation as well as a huge profit.

The rise in price was speculative, and it only partly paid off as the bonds were eventually revalued, but only at 10 pfennigs per 100 marks of the original value. In effect, investors lost 99.9 percent of their investment.

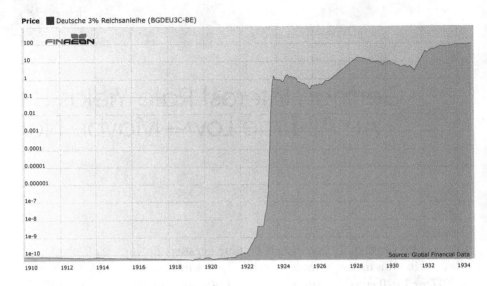

Figure 14.1 Germany 3 Percent Reichsanleihe, 1910 to 1924.

The German bonds also traded in London where the price reflected the devaluation of the currency. The value of the German bonds on the London Stock Exchange fell from 100 pounds to 5 shillings (25 pence), a loss of almost 99.9 percent.

Germans faced another default after World War II. Domestic holders of German bonds suffered losses during the currency reform of 1948 when the Deutsche Mark replaced the Reichsmark. All financial assets, including bonds and equities were revalued at 10 percent of their original value, imposing a 90 percent capital loss on German bond holders.

Foreign holders of German bonds faced a default on government bonds between 1933 and 1953 under the German Foreign Debt Moratorium of June 1933. Interest was paid in Reichsmarks into the Conversion Office for German Foreign Debts. The interest payments remained tied up in this German institution. In effect, foreign holders of German bonds were receiving no interest payments at all.

The German debts were settled 20 years later in 1953. Bond holders received about 75 percent of the value of the original bonds, the interest rate on the bonds was reduced, maturity dates were extended, and sinking funds were set up to begin paying off the loans several years later. The missed coupons were never paid back.

The "Dawes" Loan of 1924 saw its interest rate fall from 7 percent to 5.50 percent and had its maturity extended from 1949 to 1969. Interest payments were resumed on April 15, 1953, and the sinking fund was initiated on May 15, 1958. In effect, bondholders went without interest payments for 20 years and lost 25 percent of their investment. These bonds were trading at $18 in New York in

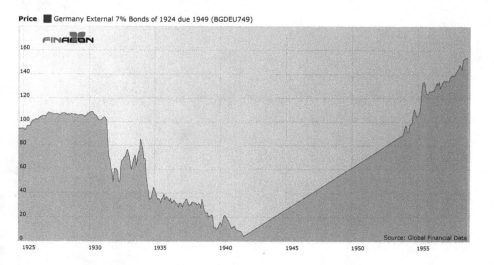

Figure 14.2 Germany External 7 Percent Bonds of 1924 Yield, 1925 to 1958.

August 1939 when World War II began, but $84 by the end of 1954 and were eventually redeemed.

Nevertheless, government bonds paying a negative yield are not going to fund a comfortable retirement for anyone. Given the experience of German investors in the twentieth century who twice suffered default from German bonds, things could be worse.

chapter fifteen

Interest Rates Hit
3 Percent—Per Day:
The Story of the Highest Interest Rates in History

The yield on the U.S. 10-year government bond reached its lowest point in history in July 2016 at 1.37 percent. Since then, yields have risen.

This raises the question, how high could interest rates go from here? Could interest rates move up to 3 percent per annum or per quarter? U.S. interest rates were that high back in 1981 when the yield on U.S. 10-year treasuries were at 15.84 percent while 30-year mortgage rates hit 18.63 percent.

We do have one case where the hyperinflation was bad enough to push interest rates up to unimaginable levels, but not so high that the whole concept of interest rates became meaningless. This occurred in Brazil in early 1990. Between 1981 and 1994, annual inflation exceeded 100 percent in all but one year, and over 1,000 percent in four of those years, with 1989 and 1993 being the two worst years. Inflation had become institutionalized in the country. Wages, salaries, prices, even bank accounts were pegged to the inflation rate, and the Banco do Brasil felt duty-bound to set a daily interest rate so people could adjust to the hyperinflation as prices spiraled out of control.

Brazil was one of the worst of the Latin American hyperinflators of the 1960s to 1990s. New currencies were introduced in 1967, 1986, 1989, 1990, 1993 and 1994. The real, introduced on July 1, 1994, finally put an end to Brazil's addiction to inflation. By the time the real was introduced, the new currency, was equal to 2.75 billion billion (2,750,000,000,000,000,000) reis, the original currency Brazil had used as a Portuguese colony. The impact of these inflations on the currency is illustrated in Figure 15.1 in the log chart of exchange rates between the Brazilian currency and the USD from 1950 to 2014.

The Banco do Brazil uses the SELIC (*Sistema Especial de Liquidação e Custodia*— Special Clearance and Escrow System) to set interest rates for the economy, just as the Federal Reserve uses the discount rate in the United States. The SELIC became

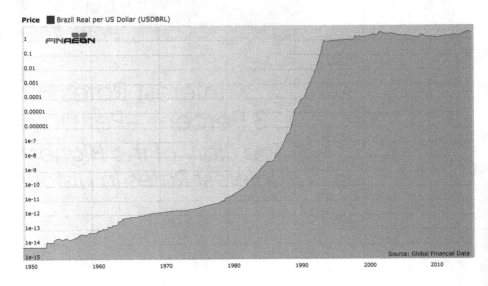

Figure 15.1 Brazil Reais per United States Dollar, 1950 to 2014.

the basis for all interest rates throughout the Brazilian economy as hyperinflation took over. At first the SELIC was adjusted every few years, then every few months, then daily. Along with the exchange rate, the SELIC became the primary indicator of inflation on the Brazilian economy.

The Banco do Brazil has a daily record of interest rates back to 1986, which is illustrated in Figure 15.2. The daily interest rates have been annualized, compounding the daily interest rates into the annual equivalent.

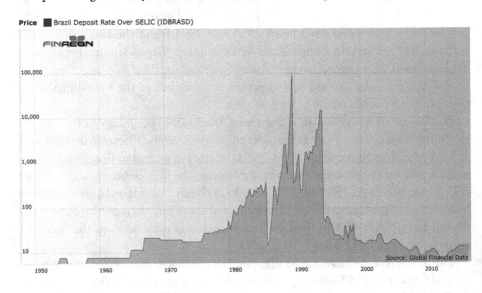

Figure 15.2 Brazil Deposit Rate Over SELIC, 1946 to 2013.

Figure 15.3 Brazil 10,000 Cruzado Note.

What is most interesting about the graph in Figure 15.2 is the exponential increase in interest rates from 1975 to 1993, rising steadily from around 16 percent to almost 16,000 percent, until the back of inflation was broken in 1993. Currency reforms are visible in the large drops in the interest rate as the government tried to reform the fiscal sector and stop the inflationary spiral, but the government inevitably returned to its inflationary fix to solve its problems.

The highest interest rates occurred in February 1990. During that period, inflation was rising at such a high and unpredictable rate, that the Banco do Brazil would only quote interest rates on a daily basis. The whole concept of annual or even monthly interest rates became meaningless, as prices steadily rose and the cruziero steadily depreciated. Daily interest rates hit 1 percent in June 1989, rose to 2 percent by November 1989, 3 percent by the beginning of February 1990, and peaked at 3.626 percent by February 19, 1990.

Although 3 percent may not seem like a lot, compounding that on a daily basis adds up very quickly. If you take the 30 days from February 1 to March 2, 1990, the product of these interest rates comes to 167 percent in one month (inflation was 75.7 percent in February 1990). If you extrapolate that on an annual basis, interest rates in Brazil hit a high of 790,799 percent on February 19, 1990. In other words, if you had borrowed $100 on February 19, 1990, you would have owed the bank $790,799 a year later. Payday loans sound cheap by comparison.

Obviously, this situation was unsustainable. The newly elected president, Fernando Affonso Collor de Mello, introduced his "shock" plan to cure the economy on March 16, 1990, closing banks for three days, the Novo Cruzado replaced the cruziero, and 20 percent of overnight market funds were frozen for 18 months. A 30-day wage and price freeze, a new wealth tax, and a widening of the tax base were introduced.

Although the currency reform slowed the rate of inflation, decreasing it from a monthly rate of 82 percent (135,000 percent annually) in March 1990 to 7.6

percent by May (140 percent annually), inflation picked up from there. Monthly inflation began its steady increase as the government continued to print cruzieros rather than raise taxes. Monthly inflation steadily increased to 47 percent by June 1994 when the introduction of the real finally put an end to Brazil's hyperinflation.

chapter sixteen

The Confederate Cotton Zombie Bonds

Confederate bonds are now prized by collectors of Confederate memorabilia. Since the bonds were never redeemed, thousands of these remnants of the South still exist for anyone to own.

One of the more interesting bonds produced by the Confederacy were the Erlanger bonds which were issued in London in an attempt to raise much-needed foreign currency for the Confederacy. These bonds were authorized by an Act of the Confederacy on January 29, 1863, and were the only bonds issued in foreign markets by the Confederacy. One of the more unusual aspects of these bonds is that they were cotton loan bonds, backed by and redeemable in bales of cotton.

The reason for issuing cotton loan bonds was that anyone who bought Confederate bonds faced the risk of default if the Confederacy lost the war. Even if the Confederate States were to survive the war, the Confederacy lacked the gold reserves requisite to back the bonds. However, the South had plenty of cotton, a commodity that was essential to the mills in England and the rest of Europe.

The cotton loan bonds were backed by bales of Confederate "white gold" at a price that would provide a profit to potential buyers if the bonds were paid off in kind rather than in cash. The £100 bonds (about $485 in gold before the war) were redeemable for 8 bales (4,000 pounds) of cotton. Additional bonds were issued at £250, £500 and £1000. The bonds paid 7 percent interest and were redeemable in 20 years.

The Erlanger bonds traded on both the London and the Amsterdam Stock Exchanges. The performance of the bonds reflected traders' faith in the Confederacy. Declines in the value of the bonds occurred as the war turned against the Confederacy, and it became more evident that the Confederacy would lose the war and be unable to redeem the bonds.

A similar indicator of faith in the Confederacy is reflected in the gold premium for the Confederate dollar. At the beginning of the war, one paper Confederate dollar was redeemable for one dollar in gold, but as the war progressed, the premium on gold rose. As you can see in Figure 16.2, the Confederate dollar depreciated

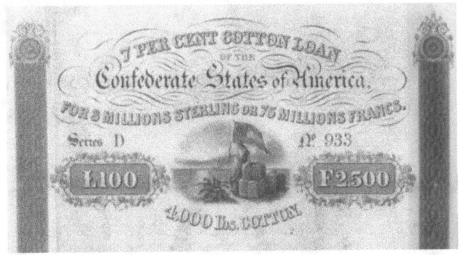

Figure 16.1 Confederate States of America 100-Pound Bond.

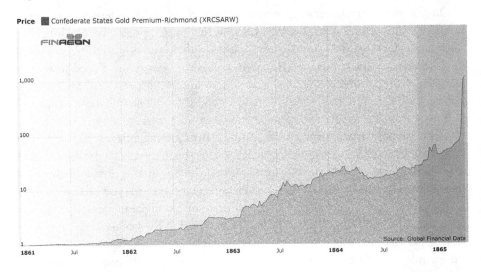

Figure 16.2 Confederate States Gold Premium—Richmond, 1861 to 1866.

consistently against gold during the war. Initially, this decline was due to inflation in the Confederacy since it was funding the war primarily through paper money and through issuing bonds. Toward the end of the war, the risk of default drove the rise in the gold premium.

The conversion rate for "bluebacks" as the Confederate currency was known, rose from 1.2 Confederate dollars to a gold dollar at the beginning of 1862 to 3.25 at the beginning of 1863, 20 at the beginning of 1864, and 60 at the beginning of 1865. By April 1, 1865, just a week before the Confederacy's surrender was signed

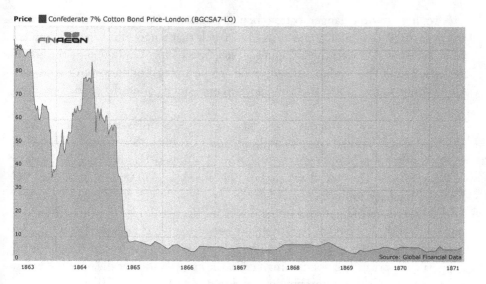

Figure 16.3 Confederate 7 Percent Cotton Bond Price, London, 1863 to 1871.

at Appomattox, the rate was at 70. After the South surrendered, the rate quickly collapsed, hitting 1500 by May 1, 1865. This can be seen in Figure 16.2.

Changes in the price of the Erlanger bonds also reflected the declining fortunes of the Confederacy. Surprisingly, the Erlanger bonds continued to trade on the London Stock Exchange for years after the war was over out of hope that the Federal government would redeem the bonds either in full or in part, or at least provide the cotton that had been promised by the cotton loan.

The United States federal government was adamant that it would not redeem any Confederate bonds, state bonds, confederate currency or state currency that had been issued during the war. The Fourteenth Amendment to the Constitution was passed on July 9, 1868 and Section 4 of the Fourteenth Amendment explicitly stated that "Neither the United States nor any State shall assume or pay any debt or obligation incurred in aid of insurrection or rebellion against the United States, or any claim for the loss or emancipation of any slave; but all such debts, obligations and claims shall be held illegal and void."

Confederate bonds became zombie bonds. Though officially dead, speculators continued to keep them alive. Since British and French courts felt that the United States government was responsible for Confederate liabilities, despite the Fourteenth Amendment, speculators in London continued to buy the 7 percent Erlanger cotton bonds. As Figure 16.3 illustrates, the price of the bonds collapsed in 1865, and fluctuated between £3 and £8 pounds from 1865 until 1871 when the bonds stopped trading on the London Stock Exchange. Thereafter, the bonds were usually quoted around £1, except between 1879 and 1884.

Two hoards of Erlanger cotton bonds remained in London after the war. Between 1879 and 1884, some bond holders felt that a new effort to wrest money from the Federal Government might succeed. Speculators began buying the bonds at 2 percent of their value, causing bonds to flow into London from the former Confederate states. When these bonds dried up, Dutch counterfeits were produced to meet the demand.

A committee was formed to make the case for the bondholders, but to no avail. By 1885, the efforts had come to nothing, and most of the bonds were returned to their owners. Some bonds remained unclaimed and these bonds settled in the vault of Coutts Bank. This hoard was sold in 1987 for over £350,000. The zombies had finally come back to life a century later.

Another hoard of bonds lay in the vaults of Erlanger Bank. This included about one-third of the bonds that had originally been issued, but not sold. In addition to this, in 1863, the Erlanger Bank had bought up some of the bonds in an effort to support their price. The bonds remained in the bank's vault for the next 100 years, surviving even the Nazi bombing of London during World War II.

In 1966, Douglas Ball, one of the experts on Confederate bonds, visited Mr. Leo Erlanger concerning the bonds in the bank's vault. The bank had been sold in 1964, and Erlanger was winding down the bank's operations. Douglas Ball, who was researching confederate bonds in preparation for his dissertation, wanted to know how many of the bonds were left. When Mr. Erlanger said they still had all the bonds, Douglas Ball let him know that he could probably make Erlanger over $100,000 by slowly releasing the bonds onto the collector's market.

Erlanger did not know exactly where the bonds were, but he was sure they were still part of the family's holdings. Erlanger called his nephew to whom he had entrusted the family papers to find out where they were and how many remained. Although Ball never heard exactly what the nephew said, after a long silence, he did hear Erlanger say to his nephew, "You did what !? How could you be so stupid!? I have troubles enough without your burning up $100,000 of my money." Erlanger's nephew, considering the bonds trash, had burned every single one, and not a single bond remained from the Erlanger hoard. A hundred years of history had been destroyed forever.

part four

Debts, Defaults, and Depression

chapter seventeen

Paying off Government Debt: Two Centuries of Global Experience

The Great Recession of 2008 led to unprecedented peacetime deficits and increases in government debt in developed countries. For only the second time in the history of the United States, government debt will soon exceed GDP. The long-run costs of and the impact of this growing debt remains highly uncertain and is one of the chief topics of political debate in the United States. While some politicians say these deficits are necessary despite the costs, others say the debts impose costs on future generations. Fiscal hawks respond by saying government expenditure must be cut.

Unfortunately, very little is known about the historical levels of government debt for different countries of the world outside of the United States and how different countries have dealt with large levels of government debt in the past. Global Financial Data has collected historical government debt and GDP data for the major world economies over the past 200 years to analyze the impact of government debt in the past.

The Origin of Government Deficits

The government runs a deficit because it is unable or unwilling to collect a sufficient amount of taxes within any given year to cover its expenditures. For most of its history, the United States balanced its budget except in war-time. After the war, the government ran surpluses to pay down the debt accumulated during the war or ran deficits that were less than the growth in nominal GDP. As illustred in Figure 17.12, U.S. debt shows rises in the Debt/GDP ratio during the War of 1812, Civil War, World War I and World War II.

The true cost to the economy of government is the expenditures it makes, not the taxes it collects. Government can either collect taxes today or issue promises (currency or bonds) to pay for its purchases in the future. When the government increases the money supply, it can cause inflation, and if it issues bonds, it can "crowd out" the private sector from the bond market.

Running deficits implies less spending in the future since the government must pay interest or retire bonds. In some cases, short-run deficits can be justified. Just as consumers or businesses may wish to smooth out the cost of consumption over time, so can the government. If the government is building infrastructure which has long-term benefits, it may borrow money and pay off the debt over the life of the project. Similarly, the government may run a cyclical deficit during a recession which it can pay off when the economy recovers.

Structural deficits are another matter. A structural deficit that is used to pay for services or transfer income, unlike capital investment, does not add to the net wealth of society and implies higher taxes or lower government services in the future to offset the accumulated structural deficits. As Robert Barro has shown, these types of structural deficits can have multipliers less than one because of their impact on incentives and the economic misallocations they create. Unfortunately, a portion of the current deficit the U.S. is running is structural in nature.

A structural deficit implies structural adjustments in the future; however, it may be difficult to generate the future surpluses needed to pay off this debt for demographic reasons. An aging population implies both a higher recipient to taxpayer ratio, and higher health care costs for the elderly. Calculations of the implied cost of the entitlement programs the government has promised in the future, such as Social Security, Medicare, Medicaid and other programs, predict large increases in these costs in the future without large reductions in the promised benefits. Any attempt to run surpluses to pay back the debt will require large increases in taxes.

Paying Off the Government Debt

Paying off the government's debt is largely a political choice. The real issue is who bears the cost of paying off the debt? Is it government workers through lower pay and lower benefits? Is it individuals who see a reduction in government services or entitlements, either directly through spending cuts or indirectly through slower growth in benefits? Is it taxpayers who pay higher taxes and fees? Are the additional taxes borne by the rich or the poor or both? Is it bondholders who get paid back in inflated currency or don't get paid back at all?

Government debt as a share of GDP can be reduced or eliminated in a number of ways.

1. Run surpluses and pay off the debt as happened in the United States in the 1830s or reduce the debt/GDP ratio by running surpluses as occurred around 2000 under Bill Clinton. Here the cost of the debt is imposed directly on taxpayers with no loss to fixed-income investors.

2. Run a deficit that is less than the growth in nominal GDP so even if you continue to run a deficit, the debt/GDP ratio shrinks. The government may have to run a surplus before interest payments in order to achieve this. The lower the interest rate, the easier this is to do. This is largely what happened in the United States between

1945 and 1973 when the debt/GDP ratio fell even though the government ran few surpluses. This imposes a lower cost on taxpayers in the short-run, but raises the total cost of debt over time.

3. Inflate your way out of the debt. If the inflation rate is high enough, nominal GDP can grow faster than the deficit reducing the debt/GDP ratio. This imposes high costs on bondholders who get paid back in inflated currency, but relieves taxpayers of the burden. A hyperinflation, such as the one that occurred in Germany can wipe out fixed-income investors. This solution works well with non-recurring debt (wars), but not with secular social debts.

4. Outright default. This can be done through a currency reform if most government debt is held domestically (Germany, 1948), devaluation if the debt is held by foreigners but in the local currency, or a default on foreign currency bonds. Here the entire cost is borne by bondholders to the benefit of taxpayers, but it becomes difficult to issue new bonds in the future.

Just as the purpose of running a deficit is to hide the cost of government services and expenditures through indirect taxation (inflation tax) or delaying the costs (issuing bonds), so the goal of the government in paying down the debt will be to make the cost as indirect as possible, or to impose the costs on those without political power.

The rest of this chapter will look at the experience of 12 major economies to see how they have created and paid off deficits in the past. Each country's experience could be the subject of a book, so only the barest of outlines is possible. Nevertheless, these brief histories and the graphs will give an idea of the choices the major Developed countries now face. We will look at both the debt/GDP ratio and Interest Share of GDP which equals the benchmark bond interest rate times the debt/GDP ratio.

Historically, several factors have caused increases in the debt/GDP ratio. The most important one is war. The primary examples are World War I and World War II. The two wars were "paid for" differently. Most governments used inflation to reduce the cost of debt accumulated during World War I and in Germany even used "inflationary default" as a way of eliminating the debt, wiping out bondholders completely. In the United States during World War II, government controlled prices and interest rates, which produced a higher return of principal in real terms but lower interest rates to investors. The debt was reduced by allowing economic growth to shrink the deficits. On the other hand, inflation in Italy and France wiped out their debt after World War II while Germany used a currency reform to eliminate its obligations.

Major recessions and depressions also increased government debt, the Great Depression of the 1930s and the current Great Recession being prime examples. Governments tend to grow their way out of the deficits generated by recessions. Wars and recessions provide quick increases in government debt, which can be reversed over time.

The final source of government deficits is the attempt to increase government benefits and entitlements faster than people are willing to pay for them. These deficits are secular in nature and generally require a restructuring of government expenditures and obligations to stop the accumulation of debt. Because of their structural nature, an outright or inflationary default is unlikely to work. Those who fear the current deficits will lead to inflation miss this point. Because of the politics involved in making these structural adjustments, reversing structural deficits is the most difficult of all.

Lenders are willing to tolerate deficits caused by war and recessions because they are temporary events that can be followed by surpluses after the cessation of war or a return to growth. Deficits that occur because of secular increases in government services that cannot be immediately reversed will inevitably lead to a financial crisis that ends in the repeal of these services.

The current growth in government debt is both structural and cyclical. Many people feel that once the government debt/GDP ratio exceeds 100 percent, a financial crisis could result. One point this chapter would like to make is that historical experience shows that it is not necessarily the government debt/GDP ratio rising over 100 percent that sparks a financial crisis, but often the interest coverage ratio reaching excessive levels because of the political cost this imposes on government expenditures. The historical examples in this chapter show that when this ratio exceeds 5 percent and investors do not see that this increase will soon be reversed, a financial crisis often occurred. Unfortunately, history shows that governments have to be forced into a crisis to solve these problems, rather than addressing them before the crisis strikes.

Australia

Australia saw its debt/GDP ratio rise steadily from 1850 to 1900 when it established itself as a Commonwealth. By 1900, the debt/GDP ratio was over 100 percent. It rose above 100 percent again during World War I and peaked at almost 200 percent of GDP during the Great Depression. Significantly, the World War II debt/GDP peak was below the Great Depression peak, though still over 180 percent of GDP. Since World War II, Australia has grown out of its debt, which now represents less than 10 percent of GDP, placing it in one of the most fiscally sound positions of any developed country.

Australia was able to increase its debt/GDP ratio through 1900 because it was a growing colony. It could borrow money in London with little problem. As it grew, Australia moved its debt burden from international to domestic borrowers and has now almost completely eliminated the foreign debt portion of its government debt. Australia borrowed as it developed its economy, and has grown out of its debt successfully with few periods of high inflation. Returns to fixed income investors in Australia have been high as a result.

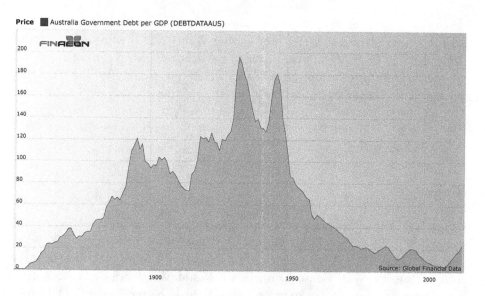

Figure 17.1 Australia Government Debt/GDP Ratio 1850 to 2010.

Canada

Unlike Australia, Canada kept its government debt relatively low until World War I, at which point it rose to 70 percent of GDP. The debt rose to over 80 percent of GDP during the 1930s and peaked at over 150 percent during World War II. The debt declined steadily until the 1970s when it started to rise again. Canada reached a debt crisis in the 1990s when secular increases in government

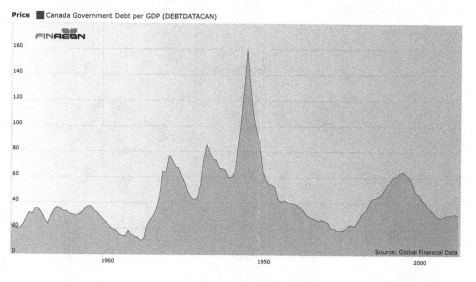

Figure 17.2 Canada Government Debt/GDP Ratio 1870 to 2010.

services and entitlements pushed debt to over 70 percent of GDP and the interest cost to over 6 percent of GDP. Even during World War II when debt exceeded 150 percent of GDP, the "interest cost" of the debt was only 4 percent of GDP.

The increase in government debt was clearly unsustainable. The Canadian government was forced to cut back on its spending to eliminate its deficits. Consequently, because Canada put its government finances in order in the 1990s, it has suffered less during the Great Recession of 2008 than other developed countries.

France

France saw rising deficits during the nineteenth century until it reached 100 percent of GDP before 1900. Most of this increase occurred after 1870 when Germany imposed a costly indemnity on France as a result of its defeat in the Franco-Prussian War. Consequently, when World War I began, France's debt/GDP ratio already exceeded 80 percent of GDP (vs. 3 percent in the U.S.). Despite inflation during World War I, France's debt/GDP ratio rose to over 200 percent by the early 1920s. Because of this debt, it is no wonder that France wanted to impose a large indemnity on Germany when Germany lost World War I.

By the beginning of World War II, France's debt/GDP ratio was down to "only" 100 percent but shot over 200 percent during World War II. With no prospect of an indemnity from Germany after World War II, France inflated its way out of its debt imposing heavy losses on bondholders, but to the benefit of taxpayers. The elimination of France's government debt laid the foundations for France's rapid

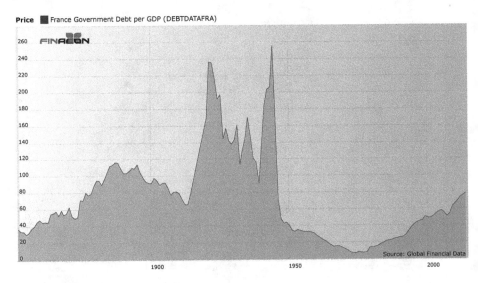

Figure 17.3 France Government Debt/GDP Ratio 1850 to 2010.

growth after World War II. Despite the fact that France's debt/GDP ratio has grown since the 1970s, it has not reached crisis levels due to high tax rates.

What is important to see about France is that after almost three decades (1915 to 1945) of low growth and having taxpayers bear a high debt cost, the government finally punished bondholders through an "inflationary default." Today, this would be more difficult to do because debt is issued in euros rather than francs or another local currency, and as we have seen with Greece, the European Union countries will help countries that could default on their debt because of the costs of the default contagion effect. But if France were to leave the European Union, the monetary union would cease to exist.

Germany

Figure 17.4 is deceiving because there are key periods, during World War I and World War II, when data on Germany's debts are unavailable. The periods when Germany's debt reached dramatic levels are simply invisible. Germany inflated its way out of its debts from World War I through hyperinflation, wiping out bondholders. In 1948, Germany used a currency conversion from Military Marks to Deutsche Mark to effectively reduce its debt obligations by 90 percent. In part, because Germany twice destroyed the assets of bondholders, it has been more fiscally responsible than other countries since World War II. Although its debt/GDP ratio has been rising since the 1970s, it remains lower than most other countries. Holders of Confederate and German bonds know that if you lend to the losing side of a war, you may lose everything.

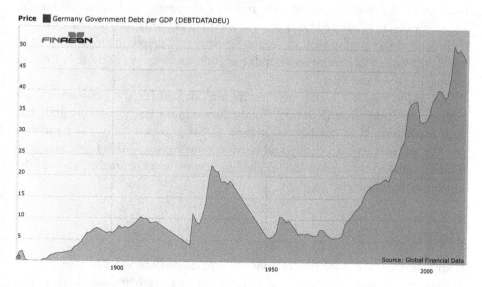

Figure 17.4 Germany Government Debt/GDP Ratio 1870 to 2010.

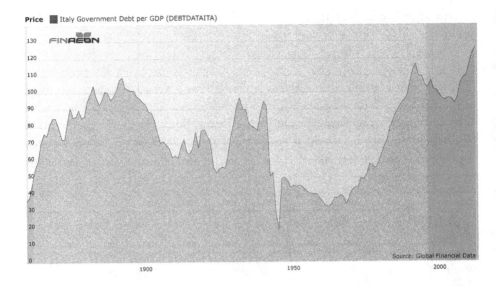

Figure 17.5 Italy Government Debt/GDP Ratio 1860 to 2010.

Italy

Although Italy has had a long history of running deficits, its debt/GDP ratio has rarely exceeded 100 percent of GDP by a large margin. Like France, Italy inflated its way out of its debts after World War II, imposing large losses on bondholders. Unlike France, it consistently ran budget deficits after World War II and used inflation as a way of minimizing the true cost. In the 1990s, Italy reformed its finances to stop the debt/GDP ratio from growing more and upon joining the European Union benefitted from lower interest rates cutting the Interest Coverage Cost of its debt to more realistic levels. Significantly, despite its high debt/GDP ratio, the yield on its government bonds has not risen as steeply as those of Ireland, Portugal, Greece and Spain.

The lesson for Italy is that persistently high deficits impose persistently high costs on investors even if the debt never hits ruinous levels. Because Italy has persistently refused to balance its budgets, it has provided the worst returns of any G-7 country to both equity and fixed income investors. This is because Italy has had consistently high inflation, yielding low or negative interest rates at the expense of bondholders.

Japan

Japan's debt/GDP history differs from other developed countries in several ways. The cost of the Russo-Japanese War in 1905 caused an early increase in debt, and as a result of the cost of World War II, the debt/GDP ratio peaked at 200 percent.

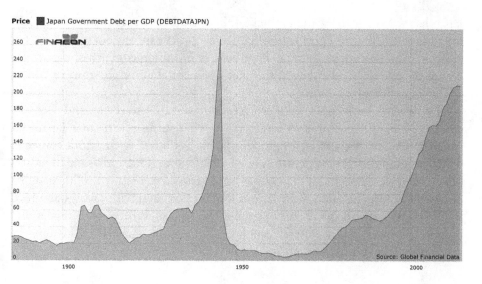

Figure 17.6 Japan Government Debt/GDP Ratio 1885 to 2010.

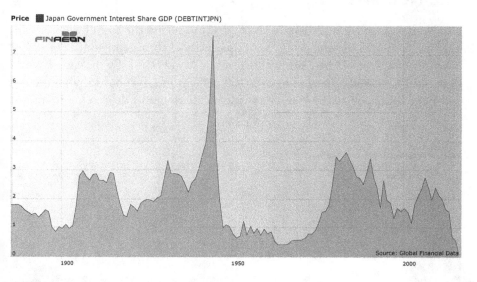

Figure 17.7 Japan Government Debt Interest/GDP Ratio 1885 to 2010.

Since the borrowing for the war was almost exclusively domestic, Japan was able to inflate its way out of its debt in the late 1940s, laying the foundations for the country's economic growth after World War II. Since the 1970s, Japanese debt has increased steadily as the country has tried to spend its way out of stagnation, reaching almost 200 percent of GDP.

Although Japan's debt/GDP ratio is over 200 percent, if you look at the interest cost of the Government debt, it was actually higher in the 1980s than it is today.

Japan has seen no increase in nominal GDP for almost 20 years, so the debt/GDP ratio has steadily risen. Japan has been unable to inflate its way out of its debt, but has paid miniscule interest rates to bondholders and absorbed much of the savings within the country. Nevertheless, the debt is structural to the government budget and will be difficult to undo.

The government's debts have crowded out the private sector and virtually eliminated nominal returns to investors. It is no surprise then that Japan has suffered two lost decades of no growth. Japan has boxed itself into a corner in which bondholders get low returns due to disinflation. If inflation were to return, bond prices would decline and inflation would reduce real returns. With an aging population, no population growth, and low interest rates with savings absorbed by the government, it is difficult to see how Japan can ever return to any level of economic growth. Every country caught in the current financial crisis would be wise not to follow in Japan's footsteps.

The Netherlands

The Netherlands had high debt in the mid-1800s due to the cost of the war with Belgium (1830–1831). The debt/GDP ratio declined consistently until the 1930s, in part because the Netherlands was neutral in World War I. By the end of World War II, its debt had increased to over 100 percent of GDP, but through growth and tight fiscal policy, the Netherlands was able to get its debt down to almost

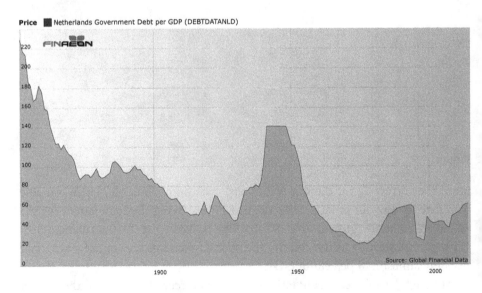

Figure 17.8 Netherlands Government Debt/GDP Ratio 1850 to 2010.

20 percent of GDP by the 1970s. With the exception of the Napoleonic Wars, when the country defaulted, the Netherlands has had no period in which fixed-income investors were significantly punished by the government. Probably, this is because of the Netherlands history as a financial center, and its status as a small, open economy.

Spain

Relative to other countries, Spain had persistently high deficits during the 1800s and defaulted or rescheduled its debt in 1809, 1820, 1831, 1834, 1851, 1867, 1872, 1882 and during the 1936 to 1939 civil war. Spain's debt rose from 60 percent of GDP in 1860 to over 160 percent of GDP in 1875 leading to a default in 1882. By staying out of both World War I and World War II, Spain was able to avoid the large debts created by these wars for other European countries. By the 1970s, Spain's debt/GDP ratio had fallen to 10 percent of GDP, but has risen since then as its social policies have changed.

Spain's debt history is different from other European countries. It had persistent deficits in the 1800s when many European countries were reducing their debts or keeping them small, then avoided the costs of both World Wars. Despite reducing its debt after World War II, adjusted for inflation, bondholders lost money between 1942 and 1985 because of rising inflation and rising interest rates. Inflation is fixed-income investors' worst enemy.

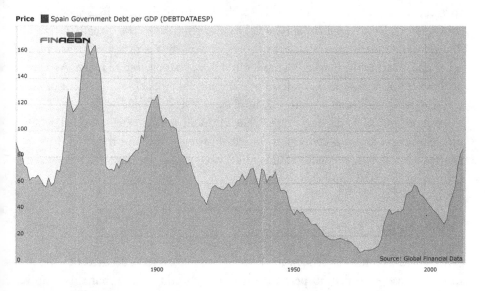

Figure 17.9 Spain Government Debt/GDP Ratio 1850 to 2010.

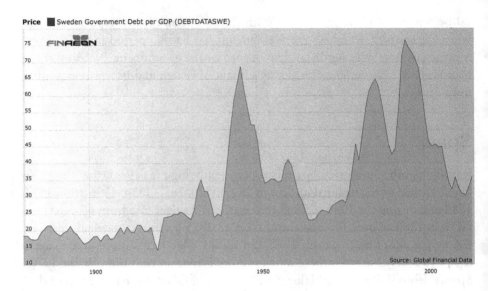

Figure 17.10 Sweden Government Debt/GDP Ratio 1880 to 2010.

Sweden

Sweden, along with Switzerland, is one of the few countries that has never seen its debt/GDP ratio rise above 100 percent. Sweden was neutral in World War I and saw its debt/GDP ratio rise to only 50 percent during World War II. The most significant increase in debt came in the 1980s and 1990s when large increases in secular social spending increased the debt/GDP ratio to 75 percent and the interest coverage to 8 percent of GDP. This sparked a financial crisis in Sweden in the 1990s, which led to a reform of its fiscal finances similar to the Canadian reforms. These financial reforms included school vouchers, privatization of pensions and other reforms that the market-loving United States has refused to make. As a result of these changes, Sweden's interest coverage has fallen back to 2 percent of GDP and the debt/GDP ratio back to the 40 percent level.

Sweden and Canada both show that entitlements can be reformed when a financial crisis forces a country to do so. However, making these reforms in a relatively small, homogeneous country like Sweden is easier than in a diverse, large country such as the United States.

Switzerland

Switzerland also has never seen its debt/GDP ratio exceed 100 percent. The only time the ratio exceeded 50 percent was during World War II, but this ratio has consistently remained below 30 percent since the 1950s. Switzerland provides a

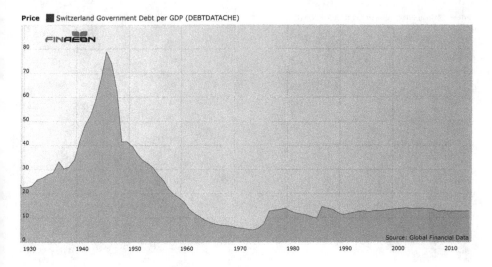

Figure 17.11 Switzerland Government Debt/GDP Ratio 1925 to 2010.

model for the rest of the world for fiscal control and the benefits of a decentralized governmental structure.

United Kingdom

The United Kingdom has the longest history of government data available for any country. GFD's data on government revenues for the UK is available since 1168 and government debt back to 1689. Both the United States and France inflated their way out of their debts of the 1700s, but the United Kingdom did not. Consequently, its debt exceeded 200 percent of GDP when the Napoleonic wars ended in 1815 and its interest coverage exceeded 10 percent of GDP. Under normal circumstances, this would have sparked a financial crisis, but in the midst of the Napoleonic wars, there were few investment alternatives and the pound sterling was the reserve currency of the nineteenth century. After the Napoleonic wars were over, the UK signaled that it would meet its debt obligations, which it did, and the debt/GDP ratio steadily declined until 1915.

The UK could not have carried such a heavy debt load had it not been the world's reserve currency and the financial center of the world. That the UK was awash with capital is witnessed by the various bubbles that occurred in the 1810s with canals, the 1820s with mining and Latin American stocks, the 1840s with railroads, and for the rest of the 1800s with the steady rise in domestic and foreign securities listed on the London Stock Exchange. The United States reaped similar benefits in the twentieth century.

Despite declining to almost 20 percent by 1914, the UK's debt/GDP ratio rose to over 150 percent after World War I and over 200 percent after World War II. Unlike

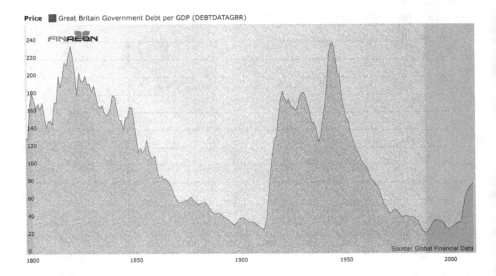

Figure 17.12 United Kingdom Government Debt/GDP Ratio 1800 to 2010.

France, Germany, Italy and other Continental countries, the UK refused to pursue an inflationary default after either World War I or World War II. London remained the financial center of Europe after World War I, and recognized the cost of an inflationary default. No doubt, the debt burden this imposed, equal to around 5 percent of GDP from the 1920s to 1970s when the UK finally went through double-digit inflation which lowered the country's debt/GDP ratio. Someone has to pay the cost of the debt, and politics determines this. Continental countries punished bondholders after World War II, but those countries' economies benefited in the long run. The UK respected its debt obligations but suffered lower growth as a result.

The UK shows both the benefits and the costs of being a financial center and having a reserve currency. On the one hand, this enables the country to borrow more as a share of GDP without sparking a financial crisis than would otherwise be possible. On the other hand, it makes it more difficult to default on debt, either through inflation or an outright default. This constrains growth in the long-run since the country is unable to reduce its debt load through inflationary or outright default. These are important lessons for the United States.

United States

The debt history of the United States is probably better known than that of any other country. The United States largely paid for the Revolutionary War through inflation with 1,000 Continental dollars converted into 1 silver dollar by the end of the war. The federal government paid off its debt in the 1830s, and despite borrowing 40 percent of GDP to pay for the Civil War, by 1915, the United States had virtually

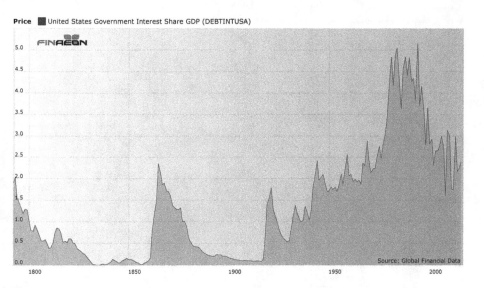

Figure 17.13 United States Government Debt Interest/GDP Ratio 1792 to 2010.

paid off its debt once again. The debt/GDP Ratio rose back to 40 percent after World War I, back to 40 percent during the 1930s and to over 120 percent of GDP during World War II, fell to 35 percent of GDP by the mid-1970s and is now around 100 percent of GDP once again. Most European countries saw their debt/GDP ratios fall between 1995 and 2008, but the U.S. ratio rose due to tax cuts, wars and expansions in government spending leaving the country with a higher debt/GDP ratio than most OECD countries when the Great Recession began.

The interest cost of covering the government's debt has consistently risen. Despite the fact that the debt/GDP ratio exceeded 120 percent after World War II, low interest rates meant that the interest coverage cost was around 2 percent of GDP. The cost remained around 2 percent until the 1970s as declining debt/GDP was offset by rising interest rates. By the early 1980s, this rose to the 5 percent level and stayed above 4 percent until the late 1990s. It was during this period of time the bond market began to impose fiscal stringency on the federal government.

The United States now faces a situation similar to Japan in which the debt/GDP ratio is rising, but the interest coverage cost is declining because of falling interest rates. If interest rates were to rise, the high debt/GDP ratio would put the U.S. in the same situation as the UK after World War II in which high interest cost coverage constrained growth. Unless there is a fundamental change to the fiscal policy of the United States, its government debt load could place it in a position of facing Japanese slow growth for a decade or two.

This problem is compounded by the fact that the debt increase is caused by secular growth in government services, not temporary military expenditures or cyclical economic fluctuations.

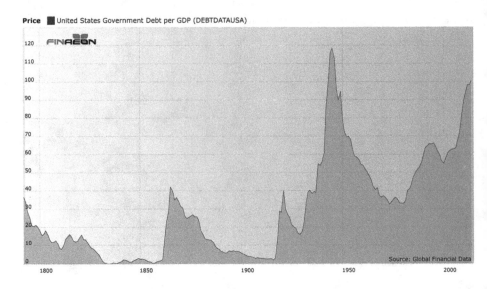

Price ■ United States Government Debt per GDP (DEBTDATAUSA)

Figure 17.14 United States Government Debt/GDP Ratio 1790– to 010.

Being a reserve currency with a financial center, as the UK was until World War II, the U.S. cannot easily default by inflation. As has been seen with Japan, if interest rates were to remain in the 2 percent range, the government's debt/GDP ratio could rise to 200 percent without sparking a financial crisis. However, as the debt/GDP ratio rises, any sharp increase in interest rates could push the U.S. into a financial crisis which would force the United States to make choices on limiting entitlements and social spending similar to what Canada and Sweden did in the 1990s.

Who bears the burden of government expenditures is a political choice. Politicians can decide to impose costs on bondholders directly through an inflationary default, currency reform, or direct default. With U.S. government bonds held so widely throughout the world, this would be difficult. However, until a crisis hits Washington, there is no incentive for fiscal reform. As long as interest rates remain low, the U.S. can pile up debt for another decade or longer, as Japan has done. Whether bondholders want to watch a slow-motion train wreck or will jump the tracks remains to be seen.

Conclusions

Our review of debt histories from twelve large countries has been revealing and can lead us to a number of conclusions.

1. There is no ceiling on debt/GDP ratios. Most of the countries we looked at had debt/GDP ratios that exceeded 100 percent without sparking a financial crisis and in some cases, the ratio hit 200 percent. Whether the increase in debt is perceived

as temporary and will decline when the cause (war, recession) is over, or whether the cause is secular growth in unpaid-for government services is as important as the actual level of debt.

2. The interest coverage cost is more important in sparking a financial crisis than the debt/GDP ratio. Japan's low interest rates have been able to sustain a rising debt/GDP ratio now at 200 percent. If the Interest Coverage rises above 5 percent, this can spark a financial crisis if it appears the level will continue to rise.

3. Even if high debt does not spark a financial crisis, high debt/GDP ratios can constrain economic growth making it more difficult to break the burden of the debt. The UK after World War II and Japan after 1990 offer good examples of this.

4. Countries with reserve currencies or countries that are financial centers can find it easier to raise money to cover government debts, but will also find it more difficult to default because of the damage it will do to its financial sector.

5. Countries that default through inflation, a currency reform or an outright default benefit by relieving themselves of the burden of the debt. The cost is that the country must reestablish itself as fiscally conservative before it can borrow again.

6. Debt/GDP and returns to fixed-income investors are inversely related with a lag. Quickly or slowly, the government tries to inflate its way out of debt reducing returns to fixed-income investors. Fixed-income investors got very poor returns globally between 1945 and 1980 after the sharp rise in debt during World War II, but superior returns between 1980 and 2010 as inflation subsided. Rising debt/GDP ratios imply low returns to investors in the future either through low (Japanese) interest rates or rising inflation, interest rates and falling bond prices.

7. Higher interest rates can spark a financial crisis that forces the government to reform, especially if the debts were created because of rising secular social costs. War debts are more likely to face inflationary default than rising social costs because the war debts are a one-time non-recurring cost. Since social expenditures largely redistribute income, governments cannot inflate their way out of these costs, but must reform. For this reason, eventually the entitlement problem, which is the basis of the current rising deficits in the U.S., must be addressed. The only question is whether this problem is taken care of immediately, or the government will wait until a financial crisis forces the government to reform its fiscal ineptitude.

8. The burden of government debt is borne by government employees, taxpayers and bondholders. Politics determines who bears the costs. With low interest rates or economic growth, politicians can continue to run deficits. Above all, politics determines who bears the costs of the government's debt. The interest groups with the least political influence are the ones who will pay the price.

chapter eighteen

Taylor's Ten: The Deficit Stops Here!

In 2008, the United States went through one of its worst financial crises in the past 200 years. The government's debt now exceeds 100 percent of GDP, and government deficits are projected as far as the eye can see. The United States is in its current situation because for the past 50 years, Congress and the president have bought votes by increasing transfers through entitlements and lowering taxes for everyone. The people receiving the transfers don't want their benefits cut, and the people paying taxes don't want to pay more taxes.

Harry S. Truman said "The Buck Stops Here." But Congress rarely stops the deficit. They might argue over how large of a deficit to have, but rarely about whether they should run a deficit or a surplus. Congress is like a bunch of drunks at a bar who buy another round of drinks so they'll have more time to decide which A.A. meeting to attend.

Taylor's Ten is a plan that will reduce the deficit while promoting growth so the United States can declare: "The Deficit Stops Here!"

Three Principles

The Tax Reform of 1986 simplified the U.S. tax system and improved its efficiency. But the financial bubbles of the 1990s and 2000s increased the revenue going to the government from capital gains. When the bubble burst, the financial crisis created the tax collapse of 2008. Instead of dealing with this problem, Congress and the president went on a spending spree, providing a fiscal solution to a financial problem. So how should Washington change things to solve existing problems and prevent future crises?

Any changes in fiscal policy should follow three principles:

1. Changes should increase economic efficiency because this will lead to growth in the economy.
2. Changes should introduce a greater role for the market to improve the allocation of resources.

3. Changes should be difficult to undo to prevent Washington from repealing changes for short-term political benefits.

Following these principles will ensure that changes benefit the American economy as a whole, and promote long-term growth for decades to come.

Taylor's Ten

There are ten changes to government fiscal policy that, when made, would follow these principles, solve the government's current deficit crisis and ensure that the economy is redirected on a path toward growth.

1. **Eliminate the corporate income tax.** Corporations don't pay taxes, they collect taxes. Any taxes they collect are passed on to consumers, workers or shareholders. The United States has one of the highest corporate income tax rates in the developed world, and eliminating the corporate income tax would do more to stimulate the economy than all of the stimulus programs passed by Congress since the financial crisis began.
2. **Eliminate tariffs.** Tariffs bring in very little revenue, but distort the economy and reduce free trade. They impose costs on the economy and only benefit those with Congressional influence.
3. **Eliminate tax expenditures.** The best way to increase revenues to the government is to eliminate the distortions in the tax code. This means removing the mortgage interest deduction and similar benefits that have accumulated over time. With the removal of tax expenditures, there is no longer any need for a standard deduction. This will expand the tax base which has shrunk to only 50 percent of taxpayers for the federal income tax.
4. **Lower marginal tax rates.** The basic principle should be that marginal tax rates should be as low as possible, consistent with balancing the budget. The alternative minimum tax should be eliminated as well. Although a flat tax is best, as long as tax rates are low, some progressivity can be included. I would change the tax break points to $50,000 and $500,000. With the elimination of tax expenditures, marginal tax rates could be lowered to 15 percent, 20 percent and 25 percent.
5. **Tax both ordinary and passive (dividends, capital gains, etc.) income at the same low rates.**
6. **Eliminate the revenue redistribution between the Federal Government and States.** If cities and states need more revenue, they should raise it on their own, not depend upon transfers from the federal government. Federal transfers allow the federal government to impose mandates on states as the cost for returning the states' and cities' funds.
7. **Require the federal government to balance its budget.** Washington should provide four-year balanced budgets. Any deficit in the current year would be balanced by surpluses in future years. Keynes never said governments should run

deficits forever, and the current system of 10-year Congressional Budget Office scoring just pushes hard decisions to a future that never occurs because of changes that undo tax and spending projections in the intervening years.

8. **Reduce discretionary government spending to 2000 levels adjusted for inflation.** The year 2000 was the last year the government ran a surplus, so cut spending back to those levels. Re-enact Gramm-Rudman-Hollings to control growth in government spending in the future.

9. **Raise the retirement age for Social Security to 70.** The minimum retirement age should immediately be raised from 62 to 65 where it was originally. Over the next 10 years, the retirement age can be raised by one year every other year until the minimum retirement age is set at 70. This would solve most of Social Security's future financial problems.

10. **Introduce progressivity in co-pays for Medicare.** The only way to control medical spending is to make people share in the cost and make them aware of the cost of prescriptions, medical services and other medical expenses. The private sector does this by requiring co-pays. Medicare should do this as well by requiring them to pay 10 percent, 20 percent or 30 percent of their medical costs based upon their income.

Never Let a Crisis Go to Waste

Congress and the President so far have been unable to solve our current financial crisis because of the intransigence of both sides. The Democrats and Republicans are like two criminals with guns to each other's heads, daring the other to pull the trigger. It's no longer "The Buck Stops Here," but "Where's George?" It's time to declare: "The Deficit Stops Here!" This 10-point plan provides long-term solutions that promote growth, and Congress and the president should work to implement them all.

chapter nineteen

How the United States Avoided Default with Only Hours to Spare—in 1895

Every few years, Congress faces the problem of raising the debt ceiling. Some support raising it, some oppose raising it, but it always gets passed.

The reason for these dramatic battles over the debt ceiling is that originally, each bond issued by the government had to be approved by Congress. When the United States entered World War I, instead of requiring that the government approve each and every bond issue, the government changed tack and set a general debt limit, enabling the government to issue new bonds at will up to the limit that was established.

It may surprise you, or probably not, but even when the government had to approve each bond issue, prior to World War I, the United States almost defaulted on its debt because of political wrangling. How shocking! This happened in 1895 when the United States was on the gold standard as Jean Strouse related in her book, *Morgan: American Financier.*

Running out of Gold

In 1895, the United States was suffering through the recession that followed the panic of 1893. Foreigners were selling their stocks and bonds and were converting their dollars into gold, which was sent out of the United States. Between 1890 and 1894, foreigners had redeemed $300 million in gold. By the end of 1893, U.S. gold reserves were down to $60 million and about $2 million in gold was being redeemed each day. By February 1894, the U.S. government had about three weeks of gold left in its vaults. After that, the United States would have to technically default on its debts because it would be unable to redeem the demand for gold that foreigners would make.

Congress was aware of this problem and knew of the possibility of default, but many representatives thought this "emergency" was being created by the money interests in New York, and in particular, J. P. Morgan, to force the government to issue bonds and put the government further in debt. President Grover Cleveland, a Democrat, knew this, but wanted to avoid default. He contacted Nathaniel Mayer Rothschild to help, who in turn contacted J.P. Morgan.

One problem was the Secretary of the Treasury, John G. Carlisle. Carlisle opposed the bond issue. He thought the bond terms provided by the New York City banks were too tough, and he wanted Congress to issue bonds directly to the public. The problem was there wasn't enough time to let Congress issue the bonds without the government going into default. Whether the bill could get through Congress was questionable.

Although Secretary Carlisle was a staunch agrarian Democrat, similar to William Jennings Bryan, he eventually responded to the economic downturn caused by the Panic of 1893 by ending silver coinage and opposing the 1894 Wilson-Gorman Tariff Act bill. By 1896, Carlisle was so unpopular that he was forced to leave the stage in the middle of a speech in his home town of Covington because of a barrage of rotten eggs. Those were the days.

Emergency Meeting at the White House

Realizing that time was of the essence, J.P. Morgan took a train to Washington, D.C. At first, President Cleveland didn't want to meet with him. Even though most members of the cabinet favored the bond issue, Carlisle was against it. In reality, the government was technically in default. There were $12 million in warrants for gold outstanding with only $9 million in the vaults. Unless something was done immediately, the United States would be in default for the first time since the Revolutionary War.

J.P. Morgan, however, had a trick up his sleeve. During the Civil War, Congress had authorized then Treasury Secretary Salmon P. Chase to issue bonds that could be offered for coin. By calling this a bailout for coin, the government could do an end run around Congress and issue the bonds without Congressional approval. Attorney General Olney investigated, found the clause was still valid, and gave his approval.

President Cleveland asked that the international bailout team of Morgan and Rothschild keep the gold in the United States. The government agreed to buy 3.5 million ounces of gold from the bailout team at $17.80 per ounce, in exchange for $62.3 million worth of 30-year bonds paying 4 percent. Since the price of gold was $18.60 per ounce, the government ended up paying $65.1 million in gold for $62.3 million in bonds, earning the bailout team $3 million. Twelve days later, the bond offer was made, and it sold out in 20 minutes.

The data for this bond shows that purchasers of the bond did well. Not only did the United States pay $3 million extra for the bonds, but the price shot up to

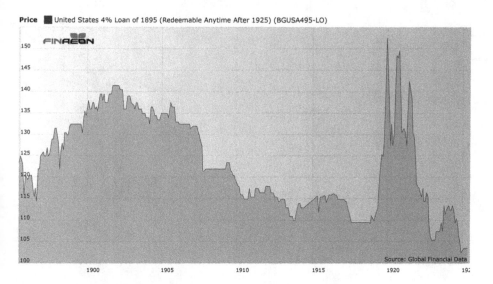

Figure 19.1 United States 4 Percent Loan of 1895, 1895 to 1925.

125 after issue, yielding 3.2 percent. In reality, the U.S. could have gotten a better coupon yield, 3.25 percent or 3.50 percent, or a better price. The 30-year bond was redeemed in 1925 at 100, trading above its par value, particularly during World War I, during the entire time of its issue.

Whether the issue is establishing a first or second Bank of the United States, issuing bonds to make sure the United States doesn't run out of gold, raising the debt ceiling to make sure the government can pay its bills, or any other government financial crisis, the players are the same. Brinkmanship is always the name of the game in politics because it gets voters' attention.

As the saying goes, I've seen this movie before. It's the Washington version of *Groundhog Day*. One hundred years from now when the U.S. government has its twenty-second-century version of potential default with only days and hours before the United States defaults on its debt for the first time, the crisis will be resolved with hours to spare as it always is.

chapter twenty

Was the Financial Crisis of 33 A.D. the First Case of Quantitative Easing?

Although many people hailed Ben Bernanke's response to the 2008 financial crisis for going outside of the box and using unorthodox policies to avoid a financial collapse, in reality, similar policies were used by Tiberius during the financial crisis of 33 A.D., almost 2000 years ago as related by Tacitus, Suetonius and Dio.

Tiberius ruled the Roman Empire from 14 A.D. to 37 A.D. He was frugal in his expenditures, and consequently, he never raised taxes during his reign. When Cappadocia became a province and provided booty to the empire, Tiberius was even able to lower Roman taxes. Tiberius's frugality allowed him to be liberal in helping the province when a massive earthquake destroyed many of the famous cities of Asia, or when a financial panic struck the Roman Empire in 33 A.D.

Financial Panic Hits the Via Sacra

As with many financial panics, this one began when unexpected events in one part of the Roman world spread to the rest of the Empire. To quote Otto Lightner from his *History of Business Depressions*, "The important firm of Seuthes and Son, of Alexandria, was facing difficulties because of the loss of three richly laden ships in a Red Sea storm, followed by a fall in the value of ostrich feathers and ivory. About the same time the great house of Malchus and Co. of Tyre with branches at Antioch and Ephesus, suddenly became bankrupt as a result of a strike among their Phoenician workmen and the embezzlements of a freedman manager. These failures affected the Roman banking house, Quintus Maximus and Lucious Vibo. A run commenced on their bank and spread to other banking houses that were said to be involved, particularly Brothers Pittius.

"The Via Sacra was the Wall Street of Rome and this thoroughfare was teeming with excited merchants. These two firms looked to other bankers for aid, as is done today. Unfortunately, rebellion had occurred among the semi-civilized people of North Gaul, where a great deal of Roman capital had been invested, and a moratorium had been declared by the governments on account of the disturbed conditions. Other bankers, fearing the suspended conditions, refused to aid the first two houses and this augmented the crisis."

At the same time, agriculture had been on the decline for several years, and Tiberius required that one-third of every senator's fortune be invested in Italian land. The senators had 18 months to make this change, but by the time the period was up, many senators had failed to make the proper adjustment. This deadline occurred at the same time as the events above, placing a further squeeze on the financial sector.

When Publius Spencer, a wealthy noblemen, requested 30 million sesterces from his banker Balbus Ollius, the firm was unable to fulfill his request and closed its doors. Over the next few days, prominent banks in Corinth, Carthage, Lyons and Byzantium announced they had to "rearrange their accounts," i.e., they had failed. This led to a bank panic and the closure of several banks along the Via Sacra in Rome. The confluence of these seemingly unrelated events led to a financial panic.

To protect themselves, banks began calling in some of their loans. When debtors could not meet the demands of their creditors, they were forced to sell their homes and possessions, and with money unavailable even at the legal limit of 12 percent, prices of real estate and other goods collapsed since there were so few buyers.

A full-scale panic followed. The panic occurred not only in Rome, but throughout the Empire. If anyone thinks that it is only in recent times that financial markets have been so fully integrated that the failure of the Creditanstalt in Vienna in 1931 or Lehman in 2008 could precipitate a worldwide panic, they clearly have not read their history. By their nature, financial markets have always been integrated, and failure in one part of the world can create the domino effect which created the Great Depression in the 1930s and the financial crisis of 2008.

Tiberius's Brilliant Response

Tiberius had retired from Rome. Although a great general, some felt Tiberius never wanted to be emperor, and he became reclusive in his later years. It took time to contact him and get a response on how to deal with the financial crisis. Several days later, he sent a letter to Rome with measures to alleviate the crisis. The decrees that had precipitated the problem were suspended. One hundred million sesterces were to be taken from the imperial treasury and distributed among reliable bankers, to be loaned to the neediest debtors. (A loaf of bread sold for half a sestertius and soldiers earned around 1000 sesterces a year, so if you take an average soldier's salary of around $20,000, you could say that one sestertius was equal to about $20 today.) The 100 million sesterces was equivalent to around $2 billion.

No interest was to be collected for three years, but security was to be offered at double value in real property. This enabled many people to avoid selling their estates at low prices, stopping the fall in prices and ensuring that the lack of liquidity never occurred. Though a few banks never recovered from the panic, most continued business as usual, and the financial panic ended as quickly as it began.

If you think about Tiberius's response, it is little different from what Bagehot would have recommended in *Lombard Street*, written in 1873, or what Bernanke did in 2008. Just as Bernanke expanded the balance sheet of the Fed, Tiberius increased liquidity by a huge amount, an early version of the TARP. Tiberius lowered interest rates to zero for three years to alleviate any additional pain, again, little different from the quantitative easing the Fed has carried out to keep both short- and long-term interest rates low.

The financial crisis of 33 AD also illustrates how integrated all parts of the Roman Empire were since the crisis involved not only Rome, but Egypt, Greece and France. It is a pity that no Roman historian wrote a financial history of the Roman Empire because it would have been fascinating. The financial panic took place over a period of a few weeks, one collapse precipitating the other, just as problems at Lehman, AIG and Morgan Stanley quickly led to problems in other parts of the financial sector and the real economy. The financial crisis was resolved with Tiberius's measures, and the downward spiral was stopped.

When Tiberius died in 37 A.D., he had a fortune of 2.7 billion sesterces, or over $50 billion. Unfortunately, his successor was his son Caligula, who was, to say the least, not as refined in his judgments as Tiberius was.

chapter twenty-one

When Charging a Lower Price Could Get You Thrown in Jail

When the Affordable Care Act was passed in 2009, one of its requirements was that everyone had to have health insurance, or pay a fine. Supporters want to keep this clause to ensure that healthy individuals who consume few health services will be part of the system and help it to stay solvent. Detractors want to remove this provision in the hope that it will hasten the implosion of Obamacare.

The problem is that given the increase in health care costs that occurs, many people may not be able to afford health care insurance and will face the prospect of paying fines for non-compliance. The whole process reminds me of what happened during the Roosevelt Administration and its ill-fated attempt to impose price controls on the economy during the 1930s. Fearing that many people would not comply with the government's regulation of the economy, the Roosevelt administration not only introduced fines but imposed jail terms for non-compliance of the new laws.

Fines for Competition

After Roosevelt became president in 1933, he introduced the New Deal to bring the country out of the Great Depression. Manufacturing production was collapsing, trade was falling, people didn't know where their next meal was coming from and unemployment lines were growing. As Figure 21.1 shows, unemployment rose from around 1 percent in 1929 to 25 percent by 1933.

After Roosevelt was sworn in as president, there was a period of two weeks in which the stock market and every bank in the United States were closed! From March 3 through March 14, 1933 banks were forced to observe a national "holiday" because too many consumers were pulling their money from financial institutions. When the stock market finally reopened, the market soared 15 percent the first day, and doubled in a few months as the intraday graph of the Dow Jones Industrial Average in Figure 21.2 shows.

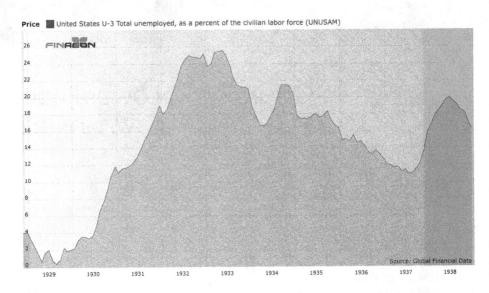

Figure 21.1 United States Total Unemployed as Percent of Workforce, 1929 to 1938.

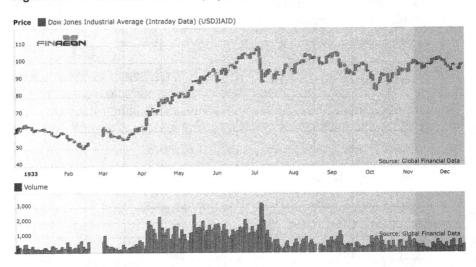

Figure 21.2 Dow Jones Industrial Average, 1933.

Some people within Roosevelt's "brain trust" felt the problem was too much competition, which was driving prices down through "destructive competition." Lower prices helped consumers but hurt producers. Roosevelt's solution was the National Industrial Recovery Act (NIRA), whose goal was to eliminate "cut-throat competition," create codes of "fair practices" and set prices for each industry. The National Recovery Administration (NRA) was set up to introduce codes of "fair competition," which would set minimum wages, maximum weekly hours and minimum prices for goods. The NRA negotiated specific sets of codes with leaders of the nation's major industries, negotiating price floors for goods and wages, and making agreements on maintaining employment and production.

With any new legislation comes a new set of government rules, and the NRA created the inevitable regulatory nightmare. Raymond Clapper reported that between 4,000 and 5,000 business practices were prohibited by some 3,000 NRA orders that ran to over 10 million pages. Businesses that supported Roosevelt's plan showed their support by putting up an NRA poster, which showed a blue eagle and the words "We Do Our Part" in their windows. If you watch an old movie, such as *Gold Diggers of 1933*, you can even see an NRA eagle that Busby Berkeley had his dancers form in the musical as a sign of Hollywood's support for the NRA.

Black Markets

As with any set of government regulations, you have to have enforcement. Black markets resulted from the NRA's regulations and in some garment districts, enforcement police were used to make sure the rules were followed. Just as the Volstead Act was passed to enforce Prohibition, each state passed laws that administered the thousands of regulations created by the NRA. The New Jersey State Recovery Act was passed by that state's legislature to make sure businessmen complied, regardless of whether they knew all the details or not.

The biggest supporters of the price controls were big businesses which, as always, were better able to apply the regulations than small firms, and which could use the price controls to increase their profits and keep smaller, more efficient firms from competing against them. In the cleaners and dyers business in New Jersey, the industry set a "fair competition" price of 40 cents for pressing a suit. Before the crash, tailors could charge 50 cents; now they were all forced to charge 40 cents.

Jacob Meged was a tailor of Polish descent who had a tailor shop at 138 Griffiths Street in Jersey City. He had a wife and four children, and he needed money to feed his family. Other tailors were charging 40 cents, but he wanted to get more business, so he put a sign in his shop window advertising that he would press suits for 35 cents. After all, this was America, where you were accustomed to being free to charge what you want. Beating the competition and being entrepreneurial was the American way, and he would be happy to press suits for 35 cents. Unfortunately, Jacob didn't get more business and instead, he was arrested.

J. Raymond Tiffany, Special Assistant Attorney General in charge of enforcing NRA codes in New Jersey took responsibility for prosecuting the tailor. When Jacob Meged was read the charges, he told Judge Kinkead that he was only vaguely aware of the existence of a code, but he pled guilty to the charge that he had violated the New Jersey State Recovery Act. Mr. Tiffany asked the court to impose a sentence stiff enough to warn other code violators that the law had teeth in it.

An Un*suit*able Jail Sentence

On Friday, April 20, 1934, Judge Robert V. Kinkead sentenced Jacob Meged to 30 days in the county jail, and he was ordered to pay a $100 fine. At 40 cents a suit, Meged would have to press 250 suits to cover his fine. That would be $100 he couldn't use to feed his family; in addition to this, he would lose a month's earnings.

As *The New York Times* put it, "He believed that the codes were designed to help the 'little fellow' and could not believe that by charging 35 cents instead of 40 cents to press a suit would put him behind bars. In court yesterday he stood as if in a trance when sentence was pronounced. He hoped that it was a joke."

It was no joke. Jacob Meged spent the weekend in jail, where he played checkers with fellow inmates. His case quickly became a *cause célèbre*, and although there is no record of it, over the weekend, political pressure was likely brought to bear upon Judge Kinkead to reverse the sentence. On Monday, Jacob Meged was called back before Judge Kinkead who remitted the fine and suspended sentence. Meged's attorney explained that Meged had been ignorant of the meaning of the NRA, and now that the purpose of the NRA had been explained to him, he was anxious to comply.

Judge Kinkead spoke to Meged like a father berating a little child. "I am glad you have come into court in a spirit of repentance.... The idea was to teach you a lesson. It never was the intention of this court that you pay the fine or be sent to prison. But there must be some way of impressing people who break the law that you did, and it is necessary to demonstrate to people that the NRA State Act will be rigidly enforced."

The jocular judge even promised to be one of Meged's customers if he raised his price to 40 cents for pressing a suit, though it is not known if Judge Kinkead ever followed up on his promise. Jacob Meged had an easy choice—shut up, do as you are told, comply, and you will be able to feed your family. Don't comply and you could lose everything. So Jacob Meged did what he had to do. He went back to his shop. He took down the poster advertising his willingness to press a suit for 35 cents and replaced it with an NRA poster with the blue eagle on it. The photo of Jacob Meged at his shop, obviously staged, was published in newspapers with the caption: "The NRA is OK." Jacob Meged also wired General Hugh Johnson, the head of the NRA, and let him know that he was "heartily in favor of it." Meged was free from jail, but not free in spirit. He had to choose between his conscience and his family, and he chose his family.

Although Jacob Meged's incarceration was the most egregious result of the NRA, there were many other examples of the agency keeping people from competing freely in the market. As a result, in early 1935, the NRA announced that it would stop setting prices. The main supporters of the price controls had been the businessmen who ran the industries. According to *Time Magazine*, of the 2,000 businessmen that worked with the NRA, 90 percent opposed the chairman of the NRA's decision to stop setting prices. Why compete with more agile, smaller firms when you can use the government to set up a cartel to protect you?

Freed but Not Free

On May 27, 1935, in the court case of *Schecter Poultry Corp. v. United States*, the Supreme Court, in a unanimous decision, held that the mandatory codes section of the NRA was unconstitutional because it attempted to regulate commerce that was not interstate in character. The Court held that the codes violated the United States Constitution's separation of powers as an impermissible delegation of legislative power to the executive branch. The Court also held that the NIRA provisions were in excess of congressional power under the commerce clause.

After the Supreme Court invalidated the NRA, Jacob Meged was free to speak his mind and indeed he did. When asked what he thought of the court's ruling, he retorted . . . "[the] NRA never was any good and is no good now." Nevertheless, the entire ordeal clearly took its toll on Jacob Meged. He became ill in 1938, went into the hospital on February 21, 1939 where he died at the young age of 54.

Reviewing this misadventure of Joseph Meged, it makes you wonder about the unintended consequences of government interference in the marketplace. Who will be the next Joseph Meged? The government has proven it is able to enforce its writ regardless of the consequences, but I certainly hope that this time, the government will leave the Joseph Megeds of the world alone.

chapter twenty-two

Cubanomics: A Nice Economy to Visit, but Even Bernie Sanders Wouldn't Want to Live There

I visited Cuba in November, 2016 a few weeks before Castro passed away, and my visit to Cuba not only provided me with the opportunity to see a country frozen in time with American cars from the 1950s acting as taxis and a vision of what a country without any multinationals would look like, but it also enabled me to understand exactly how a socialist economy worked, or as is often the case, didn't work.

Cubanomics at the Airport

Before you even leave the Havana International Airport, and perhaps without even realizing it, you are immediately immersed in Cubanomics, the upside-down Alice-in-Wonderland economic system that eleven million Cubans have to adapt to on a daily basis, and which no American would believe existed if they didn't go there themselves. Economic life in Cuba is shaped by both the desire of the Cuban government to maintain its control over the economy and the desire of the American government to perpetuate an embargo which serves little purpose except to create obstacles that can be overcome at a cost.

The very flight Americans take from Miami to Cuba exemplifies the impact of socialism and economic sanctions. Until 2016, regularly scheduled flights between the United States and Cuba were not allowed, but visitors were able to get to Cuba on a regularly scheduled "charter" flight which was really little different from a regularly scheduled flight except that it was designated as a charter so the airlines would not be in violation of American law.

When you enter the Havana airport, you proceed to immigration to get your visa to enter Cuba. Visitors have to answer several questions on the visa to assure the Cubans that they aren't bringing in any drugs, arms, pornography or walkie-talkies into Cuba, and not being a walkie-talkie smuggler, I had no worries. When a visitor goes before the immigration official, he takes your picture, for which I originally provided a big American smile, but was commanded "No smile" and so changed my disposition to please the official.

Black Market Goods Flood the Airport

Your first thought is that like any bureaucrat in any country this official has no sense of humor and therefore does not like anyone to smile, but when you realize that this bureaucrat makes about $30 per month, as do most people who work for the Cuban government, while every day thousands of dollars in black market American goods go through the airport wrapped in blue shrink wrap, you have a deeper understanding of why the bureaucrat is not smiling.

The goods brought into Cuba outnumber the luggage brought in since this is often the main way that Cubans are able to obtain American goods that are otherwise unavailable in Cuba. Some of the goods are brought in by Cubans returning from the United States, some are brought in by Americans visiting their Cuban relatives, and others are brought in by the equivalent of "consumer good mules" who run goods between the United States and Cuba.

The Cuban government controls official imports into Cuba and you never know when particular consumer goods are going to be available, or if they will be imported. A store in Havana may get in a shipment of Adidas shoes one week, but not get in any more for months. And even if Adidas shoes do come in, they are often sold out before Cubans can get the pair they want. So what is a Cuban to do? Simple, go to the Cuban version of Craigslist which provides black market access to goods otherwise unavailable in Cuba. You go to a friend who has a list of American goods that can be imported through the black market on a flash drive. Then you review the list on the flash drive and find the item you want. You then contact the person who handles that item and order what you need. They contact someone in the United States who goes to Costco or some other store in the United States and purchases the item, sends it down with a mule on a flight to Cuba, gives the item to the black marketer who then delivers it to you.

This is the Alice-in-Wonderland world of Cubananomics. If you can't buy a particular item in a Cuban store, or order it from Amazon, you can pay someone to bring the good to you from the United States. Cubans have to pay more for this roundabout way of purchasing goods, but at least they can get them. The black market fills in where there is no market, and where government regulations and American law forbids Cubans from buying what could be easily obtained at thousands of stores or online in a few minutes in the United States.

Two Currencies and No Credit Cards

After you have gotten your visa at the airport, turned in your health card, gotten your baggage and cleared customs, you can change money in the airport. Unlike other countries, Cuba has two currencies, one for the socialist economy, the Cuban Peso, and one for the tourist economy, the Peso Convertible, or cuc (pronounced "kook"). Historically, the Cuban Peso was equal to one United States dollar and provided a unified currency for Cuba. In 1985, Cuba introduced Foreign Exchange Certificates to tourists spending money in Cuba, rather than allow U.S. dollars to freely circulate. In 1994, the Foreign Exchange Certificates were replaced with the Convertible Peso, which is equal in value to one U.S. dollar, although the government does penalize tourists exchanging U.S. dollars with a 10 percent penalty which is not applicable to exchanging other currencies.

The one medium of exchange that everyone uses in the rest of the world, the credit card, is completely worthless in Cuba. No stores or restaurants or hotels accept them because the embargo places Cuba outside of the integrated financial world of modern credit. It is also extremely difficult for Cubans to borrow money from banks. Consequently, the country is on an entirely cash economy. Even if a Cuban wants to make a large purchase in the tens of thousands of dollars, it has to be done in cash.

For almost all transactions that any tourist would carry out in Cuba, purchases are in Convertible Pesos, but transactions for Cubans and for domestic goods in local stores are in Cuban Pesos. Converting from one to the other is relatively simple. There are 25 Cuban Pesos to 1 Convertible Peso so something that costs 10 Convertible Pesos costs 250 Cuban Pesos. Each currency has its own banknotes and coins that are distinguishable from each other. U.S. dollars were allowed to be used in Cuba from 1994 to 2004, but in 2004 the U.S. dollar was replaced by the Cuban Convertible Peso which is still used in lieu of U.S. dollars. Many goods are only available in Cuba by using Convertible Pesos, so Cubans have to keep both currencies in order to get what they need.

Surviving on Thirty Dollars a Month

To understand why there are two currencies, you have to go back to Cuba's Special Period in the 1990s. When the Soviet Union collapsed, Russia stopped sending the billions of dollars in subsidies that the USSR had been providing to Cuba for decades. With the withdrawal of this money, the Cuban economy nearly collapsed. In the course of a few years, Cuban GDP shrank by one-third, Cubans were without electricity for the majority of the day due to blackouts, there was insufficient gasoline for cars, and malnutrition occurred because Cuba did not have enough food to feed its people.

Until the withdrawal of the Soviet subsidies, Cuba was able to maintain the façade of having a working economy, but the Special Period turned the economy upside down and laid the foundations of the Alice-in-Wonderland economy that now exists in Cuba. The economy went through an inflationary bout in the 1990s and wages fell to their real level. Prices went up, but wages did not. Someone who had made 1000 Cuban Pesos in the 1980s when the USSR subsidized Cuba continued to make 1000 Cuban Pesos in the late 1990s, but with 25 Cuban Peso equal to 1 U.S. dollar, their salary shrank from $1,000 to the equivalent of $40.

The Cuban government had difficulty feeding its people, and rather than moving to a market economy like almost every other country in the world had done, Cuba chose to allow a very limited opening to the market in which citizens could establish small businesses, but not use the accumulation of capital to grow their business. People were allowed to work in the private sector, to open small businesses, to have U.S. dollars, to provide services outside of the public sector, but only as the equivalent of a sole proprietorship. Cuban businesses were limited to certain sectors and were not allowed to hire large numbers of people. Nevertheless, the private sector grew. Twenty years later, any entrepreneur with any business skills had left the public sector for the private sector. The rest were left to stagnate in the government sector earning an average of $30 a month.

The eternal refrain that everyone asks is, how can someone who makes the average wage of around $30 a month or receives the average pension of around $15 a month survive? You do have to understand that in addition to their salary, Cubans get free health care, free education, are provided with housing if necessary, and receive a food ration.

The Libreta de Abastecimiento provides Cubans with about 6 pounds of rice, 20 ounces of beans, 6 pounds of sugar, a dozen eggs and 15 pounds of potatoes and bananas per month (plus 1 liter of milk per day for children under 7). When available, some meat is distributed as well. After that, you are on your own.

Alternatives to Surviving on Thirty Dollars a Month

Of course, the simple answer is that you can't really survive on the government's minimal distribution of money and food. You have to find some way of supplementing the government's minimal allocation. So, what are the choices?

One solution is to leave the country and get a good-paying job elsewhere. The problem is that in order to leave the country, Cubans have to have a visa, and if a foreign government suspects that a Cuban is planning on working during their visit, then they won't provide a visa unless the Cuban is already offered a job by a company within that country. My impression is that most young people in Cuba are apolitical and only want a good job regardless of whether the job is in Cuba or another country. I think that if they had the chance, the majority of young people would leave the country for a higher paying job. Unfortunately, only the lucky ones, those with connections, or those with special skills are able to leave.

This fact was exemplified by our tour group's visit to a dance troupe which performed for us. The troupe had about 40 members in it, and when we asked if most people stay with the group or pursue other dance opportunities, we discovered that the dance troupe had a high turnover and had to hire a new member almost every week. The reason is that as soon as a dancer got an offer for a dance job in another country, they took it. If you had the opportunity of making $100 a month or less in Cuba or making $700 to $1,000 in another country, what would you do? Many of the other young people we talked to were ready to jump at the first opportunity that was offered them, if any.

The problem is that all of this creates a brain drain on the Cuban economy. There is an average of 1.2 births per Cuban woman, so the country is not replacing itself. If you then subtract out the young people who leave Cuba, there are even fewer people available to work in the economy. Then if you consider the fact that many of the people in Cuba with skills have abandoned their professional government jobs to join the more profitable tourist economy, one wonders how much longer the Cuban economy can survive being half-pregnant with socialism and capitalism.

A second alternative is to have a relative in either the United States or Cuba who will help you out financially. There is currently no limit on the amount of money Cubans in Florida can send to their family members who are still in Cuba.

The Cuban Revolution could not have "succeeded" without the financial help it gets from other countries. For decades, Cuba relied upon the subsidies from the Soviet Union. When the USSR stopped sending money, Cuba opened up and encouraged Cubans in the United States to send money to their relatives in Cuba. When Chávez came to power in Venezuela, he provided Cuba with billions of dollars in oil subsidies. Cuba continues to send doctors to countries throughout Latin America, basically renting them out for foreign exchange. But all is not well. With Venezuela collapsing, Cuba will have to avoid a second Special Period by relying upon tourism and other money for foreigners to keep the economy going. Now you know why Cuba is doing everything it can to encourage Americans to visit Cuba now that they can no longer rely on Venezuela subsidizing their failed national experiment in Cubanomics.

Cubans who don't get money from relatives in the United States can sometimes rely upon family members who work in the private sector to help them out, but the best solution to not relying on a government salary and rations is to actually work in the small, but growing, private sector. Cubans can either supplement their government salary with money earned in the private sector, or they can quit their job and work exclusively in the private sector.

Earning in One Hour in the Private Sector What Can Be Earned in a Month in the Public Sector

Before the special period of the 1990s, Cuba was like other countries where doctors, engineers, teachers and other professionals who had valuable skills earned more than those who lacked skills, but today, that is no longer the case. Thousands of doctors, teachers, engineers and other Cuban professionals have quit their jobs in the government sector to drive a taxi (often an old American car from the 1950s), open a restaurant (*paladar*), a bed and breakfast (*casa particular*) or work in the tourist sector. In one day, some Cubans can make in the private sector what they would make in one month at a government job.

Let me give you a few examples. Despite the opening up under Obama, Americans, unlike people from Canada and other countries, are still not allowed to visit Cuba on their own. Instead, they have to visit under the auspices of their visit being an educational trip, a "person-to-person" visit, or one of twelve other permitted categories to visit. To qualify for this exemption, our tour group was provided with a number of educational lectures on our trip.

Several of the lecturers came from the University of Havana. Although these speakers might only make $40 per month as a teacher, they could make $200 or more for a one-hour lecture to our tour group. In other words, they made as much in one hour with our tour group as they would have made teaching for five months at the University. Of course, without their position at the University, they would not have gotten the opportunity to lecture us and earn this large supplement to their meager government salary. Similarly, our tour guide who made about $40 a month from Havanatur, received a tip of $2,000 for the week she spent with us, the equivalent of four years' salary at Havanatur. I think you are beginning to understand the insanity of Cubanomics.

You also have to realize that none of these Cubans were "paid" by our tour group. They were either provided with a donation if they were an organization, or they were provided with a tip if they were an individual. U.S. government law makes it illegal to hire Cubans, but you can always tip or donate money and not violate U.S. government laws. Governments create regulations so people can find a way around them.

Cuban Capitalism

Most things in Cuba are inexpensive. A night at a *casa particular* is about $30–$40 and a meal in a restaurant is around $10–$20. Seven of the people in our tour group went out for dinner and had a full meal, appetizers, drinks, all for $120, about what you might spend for two people in the United States. Standard fare is fish (including lobster and shrimp), pork and chicken, and the alcohol is really cheap. You can always top it off with a Cuban cigar (no limits on bringing them back for your own consumption now). Of course, don't drink the tap water, unless you want to suffer what I call "Castro's revenge."

We were told that a waiter at restaurant might receive $200 a month or more in salary, but could make $600 or more in tips and earn $1,000 a month at a successful *paladar*. A chef could make $2,000 a month or more. Consequently, jobs in the tourist industry are in high demand and the owner of a *paladar* can call the shots. Private-sector workers in Cuba don't have the same rights as private sector workers in capitalist countries. If a worker does a poor job, they are immediately fired, no questions asked. There is no labor board to appeal to, no unemployment insurance to collect, no pension or six-months firing bonus to smooth over the transition to another job, just the opportunity to look for new employment. Despite all this, I still heard complaints that it was sometimes difficult finding reliable workers.

If you open your own business in Cuba, you can't franchise your business and reinvest your profits to grow your business. Cubans are allowed to open one restaurant, no more. Your wife can open up a restaurant, but you can't open up two restaurants. Legally, you can only have 50 seats in a restaurant, but you can call half your *paladar* a restaurant and half of it a cafeteria and have 100 seats, but you can't have 200 seats. There is a limit to the number of non-family employees you can hire, but you would be amazed at how many cousins pop out of the woodwork when the inspectors come by.

In theory, a restaurant or a bed and breakfast is in a home, and owners simply provide food to customers in their kitchen or rent out one of their bedrooms, but in practice whole houses accommodate a restaurant and every room in a *casa particular* is turned into a room for rent. To run your business efficiently, you have to have connections, not only to deal with government officials, but to make sure you get supplies of lobster and alcohol and spices and other scarce resources unavailable in regular Cuban stores. One *paladar* we ate at had salt and pepper from "Kirkland" which had been picked up at Costco on a recent trip to the United States. And of course, Cuban businesses have to deal with Cuban tax collectors who probably have little respect for entrepreneurial Cubans because they are running their own business and making money while the officials are earning a minimal salary as a government employee.

Although education is free, many young people wonder why they should spend years in college to get a professional job for which the government pays them only $30 a month when they can join the private sector and make many times that as a waiter or taxi driver immediately, or find a job in another country that pays more than they could ever make in Cuba.

At the university, there are no business classes that can lead to the Cuban equivalent of an MBA, which is what Cubans really need. All the entrepreneurial spirit is self-taught. There are even fewer opportunities in small towns. Cubans still use horses and buggies for transportation in rural areas, and there are few if any employment opportunities available, so most young people head for a larger city to find rewarding employment. Since most Cuban youth make little money, they spend their free time doing things that cost little or nothing, meeting up with others, walking along the Malecon in Havana, playing dominos or other games, and so forth. Once in a while, young people celebrate by going to a club, but only if they can afford it.

When you finally step outside of the airport building, you see the 1950s American cars that Cuba is well-known for, but of course, these cars provide even more lessons about Cubanomics. Interestingly enough, American cars in Cuba are considered to be part of the Cuban national heritage and cannot be sold to foreigners. A good car in top condition can sell for $75,000. Think of it as a capital investment in a new business. Cars in average condition can be sold for $25,000. Top condition cars are for foreign tourists and command fares in Convertible Pesos. Cars in average condition are used for locals and earn less money for their owners. It is ironic that capitalist cars are a keystone to the Cuban economy today.

But things are changing.

The millennials in Cuba grew up with hip-hop and rap just as millennials in the United States did. Cubans have been able to have cell phones and computers since 2006 and there are over 1 million cell phones in Cuba now, most of them brought in from the United States. Although Cubans don't have telephone plans that provide internet access, they can go to a hot spot, and get a password to access the internet for around $1 per hour. Then like teenagers anywhere, young people can use the Cuban version of FaceTime, text their friends, make phone calls, go onto the internet or do everything else that teenagers in the United States consider a birthright. Cuba does block some internet websites, mainly ones relating to pornography, foreign news, or employment abroad, but there is access. Cubans can get internet connections in their house, but it is horribly expensive, even by American standards.

And just think, we learned all this without even having left the Havana airport!

The Blockade: a $125 Billion Scapegoat

Once you do leave the airport, you are subjected to Cuban government propaganda. Corporations are not allowed to erect billboards advertising their product in Cuba, but the government is allowed to advertise their own product. Outside of the airport is a billboard paying tribute to Hugo Chávez (the least the country can do for someone who gave Cuba billions of dollars), protestations against the United States embargo (my favorite billboard shows a noose against black with the message: *"Bloque: El Genocidio Más Largo de la Historia"* (Embargo: The Longest Genocide in History), and the usual ones praising Che Guevara, Castro and the

Cuban Revolution. It is only upon leaving the airport that you realize what the airport didn't have: a newsstand.

Speaking of the blockade, at one of our lectures we were informed that the United States owes Cuba $125 billion for the economic costs the blockade has imposed upon Cuba. I wish the Cuban government luck in getting that amount of money out of Donald Trump.

Many people wonder how an economic system and political system that has failed its people has survived for so long, but in some ways, the answer is not that difficult. On the one hand, the Cuban Revolution was homegrown and unlike in Eastern Europe didn't collapse when the Soviet government collapsed. Castro has consistently allowed his political and economic opponents to leave the country rather than stay in Cuba. That means that anyone who has stayed in Cuba since the Revolution is not going to try and overthrow the political system. Those who are strongly opposed to Castro or who have an entrepreneurial bent went to Florida. Political opponents of the regime are still subject to arrest.

On the other hand, letting the country's critics out of Cuba and sending them to the United States has created the strong opposition to the Cuban government that exists in Florida. The former Cubans in Florida are the ones who have backed the Embargo, the special treatment of Cubans who make it to the United States, financial sanctions against Cuba, and so forth. Since Cuban Americans can't democratically oppose Castro in Cuba, they democratically oppose Castro in the United States, and since they are lucky enough to live in a swing state, they have influence over U.S. foreign policy. By getting rid of his opponents in Cuba, Castro created even stronger critics in Florida.

When we got our lecture on U.S.-Cuban relations, our tour group received a long list of what the United States had to do to accommodate Cuba, mainly remove the embargo, leave Guantanamo, end the special treatment of Cubans arriving in the United States, and so forth. But there was little about what the Cuban government planned to do to give Cubans more economic opportunities and to open up their political system.

Probably the only country with more nationalistic propaganda than Cuba is North Korea. Billboards praising Che Guevara, Fidel Castro and Raul Castro, condemning the United States and promoting the revolution with phrases like *"Hasta la victoria, siempre"* (Onward to victory, forever) are omnipresent, though I think a more accurate phrase today would be *"Hasta el turismo, siempre."* The propaganda is also on television (after a list of the wrongs the United States has done against Cuba, the TV ad encourages the United States to end these impositions with an Obamaesque "Yes we can" in English. Like any propaganda, the government's goal is to make its message so pervasive that Cubans don't even question the contrary.

Although Cuba rails against the Embargo, I wonder what the Cuban government would do if they no longer had the United States as a scapegoat to blame their problems on. After all, there are over one hundred other countries in the world that can invest in Cuba, send tourists, freely import and export goods and help the Cuban economy to grow. To blame the United States for all that is wrong with Cuba simply avoids the question of what Cuba has done wrong, and what changes Cuba needs to make for its citizens to improve their standard of living in the absence of any change from the United States. With China and Eastern Europe successfully shaking off the shackles of socialism and enriching their own people, there is no reason why Cuba couldn't do the same.

There is No Such Thing as "One" Starbucks

Yet, many Cubans still don't understand what capitalism is all about. One of our lecturers told us they were in favor of allowing in foreign firms as long as they allowed Cubans to maintain 51 percent ownership. We asked about having Starbucks in Cuba and our lecturer said he thought Cuba should allow "one" Starbucks in Havana. Obviously, the professor just didn't understand that there is no such thing as "one " Starbucks.

All the Cubans we met were free and happy to answer any questions we had. Everyone in Cuba seems to know someone in the United States or Mexico or another country, so they know what life is like outside of Cuba. But how the government can continue to do a balancing act between Cubans who earn virtually nothing when working for the government and those in the private sector who earn many times what their fellow government employees make is a dialectical tension that can't go on forever.

I had a great time in Cuba and had an economics lesson that I could never have received anywhere else. Although many people go to Cuba to see the old cars from the 1950s, treat your visit to Cuba as a unique lesson in Economics. As one of our fellow travelers told me, "I never appreciated Capitalism until I visited Cuba."

Even Castro is said to have admitted to a foreigner that "the Cuban model doesn't even work for us anymore." But if socialism failed in Venezuela which had no embargo and billions of dollars in oil, in China with a billion people and extensive resources, or in the Soviet Union which established a Marxist legacy for the world, why would socialism succeed in a Cuba? The truth is that without the billions in foreign subsidies from the Soviet Union or Venezuela or Florida émigrés, the Cuban economy would have collapsed decades ago. Now that Fidel Castro has died, we will see whether the Cuban Revolution was more about Castro than about Communism.

part five

The Equity Risk Premium

chapter twenty-three

Ten Lessons for the Twenty-First-Century Investor

What lessons can we learn from the behavior of the world's financial markets in the twentieth century that are useful to investors in the twenty-first century? The 10 points below cover some of the most important lessons we have gained from studying a century of data on financial markets.

1. Stocks Outperform Bonds and Bills Over the Long-Term

In every country that we surveyed, stocks beat both bonds and bills over the long-term. The equity premium, the difference between the return on stocks and bonds, is usually positive. There were some decades in which bonds outperformed stocks, but those decades were the exception, not the rule.

The primary reason for the equity premium is that equities are riskier than bonds. Shareholders are only paid after all suppliers, employees, and creditors are paid. This makes equity prices more volatile than bond prices, and shareholders must be compensated for this additional risk. Since bonds are loans, and interest rates depend upon the supply and demand for capital, returns to fixed-income investments are not directly related to the growth in the economy. When economies grow, as they have during the past 50 years, investors received superior returns as compensation for the risks they took. This important fact will remain true in the twenty-first century.

2. Equity Risk Premium or Inflation Risk Discount?

Though it is clear that equities outperform bonds over the long run due to the higher risk that shareholders face, this says nothing about how much of an equity risk premium investors should receive. The equity risk premium suffered dramatic swings during the twentieth century. Even though, on average, the equity-bond premium was around 4 to 5 percent, in some years, the equity-bond risk premium was 30 percent or greater, and in some cases it was a negative 20 percent or worse.

One reason for this is that different factors drive returns on stocks and bonds. Stocks are primarily driven by expectations of future earnings, and government bonds by expectations of future inflation. Equity prices and dividends adjust to inflation rates over time, but secular increases or decreases in inflation affect returns to fixed-income investors

3. The Return on Stocks and Capital Gains Increased During the Twentieth Century

Returns to investors were higher after World War II than before World War II, primarily because of higher capital gains, not because of higher dividend yields. Investors received higher capital gains after World War II, even after adjusting for inflation. The period since World War II has provided the economically stable environment needed to improve corporate profits and allow investors to earn higher returns.

4. The 1950s Were a Turning Point for Investors in the Twentieth Century

The period from 1914 to 1949 was one of substantial economic and political problems throughout the world. Two World Wars and the worst economic downturn of the century occurred during this period of time. The period began with World War I, and ended with the beginning of the Cold War after Germany was separated into two halves and the Bretton Woods system was established.

This leaves us with an important question. Will investors in the twenty-first century continue to benefit from a stable economic and political environment as existed between 1949 and 1979, or will there be a period, like 1914 to 1939, when investors suffer for decades?

5. Past Performance is No Guarantee of Future Returns

There is a good reason for this clichéd disclaimer. Our survey of returns to stocks, bonds and bills shows that returns during the recent past are rarely a good predictor of what returns will be in the future. We found that time and time again, periods in which investors had the greatest returns were often followed by periods in which investors had their worst returns and vice versa. What proved to be the right choice in one decade, proved to be the wrong choice in the next decade. This is simply the nature of financial markets, and there is no reason to expect that this fact of life will change in the future.

6. Inflation is the Greatest Enemy of Investors

The greatest declines in real stock market returns during the twentieth century occurred during periods of extreme inflation. Both Germany and Japan saw real equity prices decline by over 95 percent during the inflations that followed World War I and World War II, respectively. The only decade in the twentieth century in which none of the world's major stock markets provided positive real returns was not the 1930s, but the 1910s when the unexpected inflation caused by World War I exceeded the increase in stock market prices worldwide. Similar inflationary periods, such as the late 1940s or the 1970s generated poor returns to investors throughout the world.

7. Government Policies are Extremely Important to Financial Markets

Whether the government's policies create stable economic and political conditions in which corporations can invest in order to increase productivity and earnings, or whether there is political and economic uncertainty strongly affects returns. Countries such as the United States, Switzerland, Sweden and Australia that were stable for most of the twentieth century, provided good opportunities for consistent total returns to investors who sought a buy-and-hold strategy. Investors in countries where political and economic uncertainty occurred saw dramatic swings in the values of their portfolios. Governments that pursued policies that generated high inflation rates imposed heavy losses on investors.

8. Stocks, Bonds and Bills Do Not Guarantee a Positive Return in the Long Run

Most of the research on long-term returns has been done in the United States since World War II. Data on returns during this period of time can be misleading because the data come from an economy that provided the best economic and political environment for strong returns on stocks in the last half of the twentieth century. The United States has been studied because good data are available on the stock market; however, this is a biased sample.

Every one of the G7 countries suffered at least one period in which equities lost 75 percent of their market value, and most countries saw similar losses of 75 percent or more in bonds and bills when inflation reduced real returns to fixed-income investors. Should we believe that this is not going to be repeated in the century that follows?

9. Buy-and-Hold Can Work in a Stable Economic and Political Environment; Otherwise, Market Timing is Recommended

Research on the United States stock market has shown that a buy-and-hold approach to stocks can be a good choice for long-term investors. According to this view, trying to time the market and determine exactly when the market has hit bottom or topped out is a fool's game.

What has gone unrecognized is the fact that one reason for the superiority of buy-and-hold investing in the United States is the relatively stable economic and political environment that prevailed in the United States during the twentieth century. With a few exceptions, bear markets in the United States were short and relatively mild compared to bear markets in other countries. Despite some severe setbacks, the long-term trend in American stocks was generally upward throughout the twentieth century.

Because individuals have a stake in their stock market's performance, they will place even greater demands on governments to follow policies that allow corporations to provide the earnings growth necessary to generate strong stock market returns. Otherwise, unless investors are good market timers, the only choice investors have is to avoid these countries completely.

10. Emerging Markets Provide the Greatest Opportunities for Gains—and for Losses

The most dramatic bull markets in the twentieth century occurred in emerging markets. The most dramatic bear markets of the twentieth century occurred in emerging markets. Chile's stock market increased 60-fold, in real terms, between 1973 and 1980. The Mexican stock market increased almost 30-fold between 1982 and 1987 in real terms. Other Latin American markets saw 10-fold real increases at one time or another during the past 20 years. On the other hand, Peru had the worst performance of any of the world's stock markets between the 1940s and the 1980s, losing 99 percent of its value in real terms. When emerging markets get hot, the reward can be overwhelming, but once they falter, losses can pile up quickly.

Conclusion

What about the century to come?

No one at the beginning of the 1900s would have predicted the roller-coaster ride that investors went through in the twentieth century. Almost every assumption that investors at the beginning of the twentieth century held to be true proved false. In some countries, investors lost everything they had during the last century. In others, inflation slowly destroyed their portfolios. Countries where businesses enjoyed stable economic environments that enabled them and their investors to profit were the exception, not the rule.

The period from 1914 to 1949 was terrible for investors. The period from 1949 to 1999 were the best 50 years for investors in human history. Which of these two periods will characterize the twenty-first century?

It is impossible to know whether World War III, new bouts of inflation, terrorism or other factors that create economic and political chaos will condemn investors to lower returns in the future. Was the last half of the twentieth century the framework for what will happen in the twenty-first century, or was it an interlude between periods of war, inflation, protectionism and international uncertainty?

We do not know. What we do know is that the twentieth century has provided us with every possibility that investors can face from decades with dramatically high returns to decades that wiped out investors. We know what works and what doesn't work.

In the twenty-first century, people will live longer. They will be retired longer, and this will create a greater need to save for retirement. Investing in financial assets only works if there are stable economic, political and financial conditions that enable investors to earn consistent returns from their investments. Hyperinflation, government defaults, war, economic and political instability, government barriers to free trade all wipe out investment portfolios. Germans in 1923 and in 1948 had to start from scratch. Investors in the future don't want to be put in that situation.

Every decade in the twentieth century presented new challenges to investors. What worked for investors in one decade rarely worked in the next decade. The lesson to be learned here is that investors must be eternally vigilant in the century to come. They should never take investing for granted. The economy, technology and government policies are constantly evolving, and so will financial markets and the returns they generate. We may not be able to predict the future, but we can study the past to better understand how to respond when changes occur.

Welcome to the twenty-first century.

chapter twenty-four

The Equity Risk Premium

The equity risk premium, the rate by which risky stocks are expected to outperform safe fixed-income investments, such as U.S. government bonds and bills, is perhaps the most important figure in financial economics. The equity risk premium indicates how much more an investor should expect to earn by investing their money in the stock market than in government bonds. If the equity premium is high, people should allocate more of their portfolio to stocks; if it is low, then more to bonds.

Investors must examine the past to discover what has already happened, and form expectations about what they believe is going to happen in the future. This article provides information about the past and how investors may use this information to form conclusions or expectations about future returns.

What Determines the Equity Risk Premium?

Let's assume that investors can put their money into cash, bonds or stocks. What rate of return should they expect from each? The return to a safe, long-term investment should equal the rate of growth in the economy. Investors will demand compensation for giving up access to their funds. If historically, GDP has grown at 5 percent in nominal terms, then the return to risk-free bonds should also be 5 percent. Corporate bonds offer additional risks because they face default risk, and even AAA corporate bonds yield about 1 percent more than U.S. Government Treasury bonds. Shareholders face the greatest risk because they are residual owners in the firm and are paid last. The equity premium measures the additional returns to stocks that shareholders receive to compensate them for the high level of risk they face.

For fixed-income investors, the primary risk they face is inflation. Rising inflation in the United States in the 1960s and 1970s hurt bond investors, reducing real returns on bonds to zero. For equity investors, the primary risk is lower corporate earnings and the expectation that there will be lower earnings in the future. The optimal situation for investors is one of declining inflation (raising the returns to bondholders) and rising earnings (increasing the returns to shareholders).

In short, rational investors must try to predict future inflation, the future growth in the economy, and future corporate profits in order to determine how to best invest their money.

Estimating the Equity Risk Premium over Time

Although it may be beneficial to know what returns have been to stocks and bonds over the past 50 or 100 years, few people invest for a 50- or a 100-year period. Individuals who are investing for their retirement would be more likely to invest for a 20- or 30-year time period, saving money in their 30s and 40s, and drawing the money out in their 60s and 70s. Hence, a review of returns and the equity risk premium over 30-year holding periods would probably give investors a more objective estimate of what they could expect in the future. Table 24.1 provides an interesting perspective on how the returns to stocks and bonds have changed over

Table 24.1 The Equity Risk Premium for 30-Year Holding Periods

Ending Year	30-year Return on Stocks (Percent)	30-year Return on Bonds (Percent)	30-year Equity Premium (Percent)	30-year Average Inflation Rate (Percent)
1871–1901	6.64	4.37	2.18	0.36
1881–1911	5.85	3.24	2.53	0.60
1891–1921	5.88	3.27	2.53	2.89
1901–1931	5.26	3.42	1.77	2.18
1911–1941	5.23	3.95	1.23	1.64
1921–1951	9.47	3.38	5.90	1.43
1931–1961	12.89	2.68	9.96	2.43
1941–1971	13.34	2.56	10.51	3.30
1951–1981	9.91	3.06	6.64	4.31
1961–1991	10.26	7.45	2.61	5.22
1971–2001	12.25	8.71	3.26	4.98
1981–2011	10.96	9.77	1.09	2.96
1986–2016	10.37	6.37	3.76	2.89

time in the United States. Although investors in the 1920s to 1950s enjoyed a high equity risk premium, in most other decades it was around two to three percent.

Why Did the Returns to Stocks and Bonds Change in the Past?

There were two stages in the changes to investment returns. The first change was an increase in the returns to equities, beginning in the 1950s. This increase came primarily through higher capital gains rather than through higher dividends since dividends have actually decreased over time. Throughout the 1970s, the nominal 30-year return to bondholders was less than the inflation rate over the previous 30 years. The combination of these two factors produced a sharp increase in the equity risk premium, pushing it over 10 percent by 1971.

The second change occurred when Paul Volcker began to attack inflation in the early 1980s, bondholders saw sharp increases in their returns. The increase in the return to bonds reduced the equity premium and allowed bondholders to once again receive returns that exceeded the inflation rate. For investors today, the question they should ask themselves is what they expect to happen in the next 10, 20 or 30 years. Will the economy return to the conditions of the 1950s and 1960s when there was rising earnings and rising inflation that favored equities, or lower earnings and lower inflation that favored bonds, or to a more stable environment of steady growth and inflation?

10 Rules to Remember About the Equity Risk Premium

Based upon our analysis of the returns to stocks, bonds and bills over the past 145 years, we have been able to formulate some general rules for determining how to allocate assets over different time horizons and different economic situations. These rules should prove invaluable to investors.

1. Bonds beat bills unless there is a bear market in bonds due to rising interest rates (the 1970s).
2. Stocks beat bonds unless there is a bear market in equities due to declining earnings or expectations of declining earnings (the 1930s).
3. The best returns to investors occur in periods of disinflation and rising earnings (the 1980s).
4. The worst returns to investors occur in periods of rising inflation and falling earnings (the 1910s).

5. The equity risk premium is maximized in periods of rising inflation and rising earnings (the 1950s).

6. The equity risk premium is minimized in periods of disinflation/deflation and falling earnings (the 1930s).

7. Variations in the risk premium, even over investment periods of 30 years, is so great that the average risk premium is irrelevant.

8. The current equity premium over the past 10 or 30 years provides no predictive capacity over the future equity premium.

9. There is mean reversion to the equity risk premium. Years when the equity premium is high (1971, 1999) are the worst periods to invest in equities, and years when it is low (1981) are often the best.

10. The four things that determine the future value of the risk premium are the future inflation rate (which determines nominal bill returns), the future growth rate of the economy (which determines bond returns), the future growth in corporate profits (which determine stock returns) and investor expectations of these variables.

chapter twenty-five

The Golden Age of Investing, 1974 to 2004

Few investors realize it, but the period between 1974 and 2004 was a Golden Age of Investing. During those thirty years, investors throughout the world received the highest returns on a diversified portfolio of stocks and bonds in history.

Given the current global debate on the future of social security, pensions and personal retirement accounts, it is important to understand how this Golden Age took place and whether it will occur again. Investors want to know not only what future returns to stocks and bonds are likely to be, but whether stocks will do better than bonds, and how much risk they will face if they choose to invest in stocks rather than in government bonds.

Investment Returns Between 1974 and 2004

How should we analyze historical returns on financial assets? People invest for different periods of time, some may day trade, others may hold stocks and bonds in their retirement account for decades. Most analyses of historical returns calculate annual returns and then calculate risk based upon these annual holding periods. However, few people invest for only one year. Long-term investors are more interested in finding out the risks and returns to stocks for longer periods of 10 or 30 years, rather than for one year.

Using data from 1925 to 2004, we analyzed all 1-year, 10-year and 30-year returns to stocks, as measured by the S&P 500, 10-year government bonds, and 3-month treasury bills over the past 80 years. We made similar calculations for the other G7 countries and for three global indices. A summary table for these data is provided in Table 25.1.

Stocks are represented by the broadest index of stocks in each country, bonds by 10-year government bonds and bills by 3-month treasury bills.

Table 25.1 Annual Real Returns 1974 to 2004

	Stocks	Bonds	Bills	Portfolio
Australia	9.46	5.36	3.32	7.41
Canada	6.89	5.71	2.77	6.33
Europe (USD)	9.19	4.43	1.76	6.81
France	8.95	5.97	3.08	7.46
Germany	6.42	4.18	2.72	5.3
Italy	5.06	5.48	5.57	5.27
Japan	4.04	5.1	1.31	4.57
United Kingdom	10.7	5.02	2.49	7.86
United States	8.93	4.43	1.76	6.68
World (USD)	7.91	4.43	1.76	6.17
World x/USA (USD)	7.98	4.43	1.76	6.21

The portfolio represents an investment of 50 percent in stocks and 50 percent in bonds. Returns for individual countries are in local currency after adjusting for inflation. Returns for international indices are all in USD after inflation.

Analyzing asset returns using holding periods of 10 and 30 years, rather than 1 year, produced two important conclusions that were not readily apparent using shorter holding periods.

First, using longer holding periods, we found little difference in the relative returns to stocks and bonds, but significant differences in investors' risk-reward tradeoff. Second, we discovered that the period from 1974 to 2004 provided investors with the best returns in history.

For holding periods of 10 or 30 years, not only did shareholders on average receive a higher return than bondholders, but they faced less risk as well, especially over a 30-year horizon. The argument that retirement accounts investing in equities, rather than government bonds, increase the risk to retirees is simply not true for holding periods of 10 years or more.

In the United States, stocks have provided an average annual return of around 7 percent after inflation during the past 80 years. The standard deviation (risk) is about 18 percent using annual data, 5 percent using 10-year investment periods and only 1.4 percent using 30-year investment periods. The only time in U.S. history when stocks provided negative real returns over a 10-year period was the late 1930s. Stocks have never provided a negative real return over a 30-year period, even after adjusting for inflation. Longer holding periods clearly reduce risk.

Government bonds beat inflation by about 2 percent over the same period of time, but the ratio of risk to return is higher for bonds than for stocks for 10- and 30-year holding periods. From the 1940s to the 1970s, government bond returns failed to beat inflation.

Why do equities face less risk than government bonds in the long run, but not in the short run? The answer is simple. Equity returns are sensitive to earnings expectations, while government bond returns are sensitive to inflation expectations and to rising interest rates. In any given year, earnings expectations can vary more than inflation and interest rate expectations, but over long periods of time, earnings recover as do stocks.

The United States has faced several decades of rising and fluctuating rates of inflation (from the 1930s to the 1970s), but never several decades of falling earnings. Hyperinflations and long-term inflation can wipe out fixed-income assets, but earnings adjust to inflation.

The two best 30-year investment periods for equities in the United States were from 1931 to 1961 and from 1974 to 2004. The story for fixed-income investors was quite different. Between 1931 and 1961, bondholders barely beat inflation. Between 1974 and 2004, they received a 4 percent annual real return.

What was unique about the period from 1974 to 2004 was that both stocks and bonds provided investors significant real returns. In the past, there were periods when stocks or bonds did well, but there had never been a similar 30-year period when all financial assets provided such high returns.

These results occurred in other countries as well. Between 1974 and 2004, Australia, Canada, Europe, Italy and the United Kingdom, as well as World and European indices all provided the highest returns to portfolios of stocks and bonds for any 30-year time period over the past 80 years. The only exceptions to this rule were Japan and Germany.

This is an important discovery. What caused returns to financial assets over those 30 years to be the greatest in history? What went right? And more importantly, can today's investors look forward to another Golden Age over the next 30 years?

What Went Right

There are two reasons why investors enjoyed such high returns. First, stocks and bonds both had low valuations in 1974 providing opportunities to investors as the economy and the investment climate improved. Second, during those 30 years governments pursued economic policies that fought inflation (increasing returns to bonds) and promoted international trade and economic growth (increasing returns to equities).

Investors in 1974 would have seen little reason to invest in either stocks or bonds. The bear market of 1973–1974 was the worst since the Great Depression and the yield on 10-year U.S. Government bonds exceeded 8 percent for the first time in history. Inflation was rising as commodity prices, especially oil, shot up in price after price controls had failed. The Bretton Woods system of fixed exchange rates had collapsed after 25 years, breaking the link between the USD and gold. Political uncertainty over Vietnam, Watergate, the Middle East and elsewhere added to the general economic malaise. It is not surprising that someone in 1974, looking to retire in 2004, would have been wary of investing in either stocks or bonds, but this was exactly what an astute investor should have done.

After 1974, much went right. Central banks throughout the world gained their independence from governments and brought inflation down. The experience of the 1970s showed that Keynesian fiscal policy led to higher inflation, not lower unemployment and higher rates of growth. The decline in nominal interest rates after 1981 generated capital gains and interest income for bondholders. This reversed the trend of rising interest rates and capital losses that plagued bond investors from 1940 to 1981.

At the same time, globalization, the spread of capitalism to socialist and communist countries, the integration of regional economies in Europe, the international reduction in trade barriers, the incredible technological changes in electronics, biotechnology and the internet, as well as countless other changes have all raised economic growth and corporate earnings.

Average earnings for the S&P 500 increased seven-fold between 1974 and 2004. Not only did corporate earnings rise, but the improving global economy and increased opportunities raised investor confidence. The average price-earnings ratio more than doubled during this period, adding to equity returns.

What went right for investors was the combination of rising inflation and economic malaise in 1974 being replaced by low inflation and economic growth. The fall in inflation rates and interest rates, combined with the increase in investor confidence, and thus the price-earnings ratios added to these returns as never before (Figure 25.1).

Will the Golden Age Continue?

Investors today face one disadvantage relative to investors 30 years ago. Long-term interest rates are lower today and the valuation of the stock market is higher than in 1974. This will prevent investors from benefiting from the falling interest rates and rising P/E ratios between 1974 and 2004

This does not mean that investors today cannot receive good returns over the next 10 or 30 years. There are immense opportunities awaiting corporations that would enable corporate profits, and thus stock prices, to increase over the next 30 years.

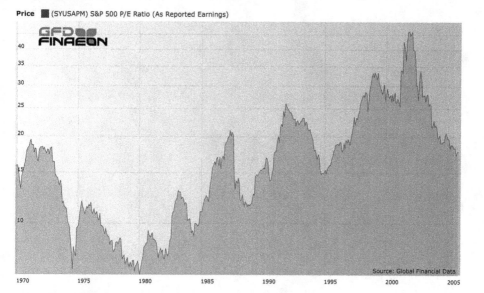

Figure 25.1 S&P 500 P/E Ratio, 1970 to 2005.

The lesson of the Golden Age of Investing is that government policies that fight inflation, that promote international trade, technological change and economic growth benefit investors. China, India, Eastern Europe and Russia have joined the world economy, adding three billion people to the global market. This should be viewed as a great opportunity for the world, not a challenge to it. In biotechnology, electronics and other areas of technology, unknown new products await development.

During the next 30 years, retirees will rely more and more on their returns from stocks and bonds for their retirement income. This makes it all the more important that governments worldwide allow markets the freedom they need to generate economic growth, rising profits, and higher returns to equities.

Investors today may not be able to enjoy the Golden Age returns between 1974 and 2004, but if governments pursue non-inflationary, free market policies, investors may be able to look forward to a Silver Age of high investment returns.

chapter twenty-six

Have the Financial Markets Given a Once-in-a-Generation Signal?

One of the principal decisions investors have to make is how to allocate their assets between stocks and bonds. Although stocks generally provide a higher rate of return than bonds, stocks are also more volatile, and investors run the risk that when they need to take money out of their portfolio, stocks might be in a bear market, reducing the amount of money available to them.

One of the indicators we look at, in order to determine the optimal allocation between financial assets, is the relative returns between stocks and bonds, and in particular, the 10-year and 20-year rates of return to stocks and bonds. We have found these to be one of the most effective indicators for allocating assets. Five-year rates of return have too much noise in them to provide useful signals, and 30-year rates are too stable to provide important signals on the relative returns on stocks and bonds. We use the return on the S&P 500 for stocks and the GFD's index of returns on 10-year government bonds for bonds.

As most investors know, stocks generally outperform bonds over time because equities are riskier than bonds, and investors must be compensated for this risk with a higher rate of return. However, this is not always true. Occasionally, though rarely, bonds outperform stocks over a period of 10 or 20 years. This only happens once in a generation, and the Financial Crisis of 2008 created one of those rare events. As a result of the financial crisis, for the first time since the 1970s in the United States, stocks underperformed bonds over the previous 10 years, and for the first time since the 1940s, stocks underperformed bonds over the previous 20 years.

Typically, investors look at the annual returns to stocks, bonds and bills and the volatility of returns to determine the level of risk they face in choosing between assets. In reality, investors don't look at one-year time periods in making their long-term investment choices, but want to look at periods of ten, twenty or more years in order to prepare for their retirement. Without a long set of data, there is insufficient evidence to make informed decisions about how to allocate investment resources between different asset classes.

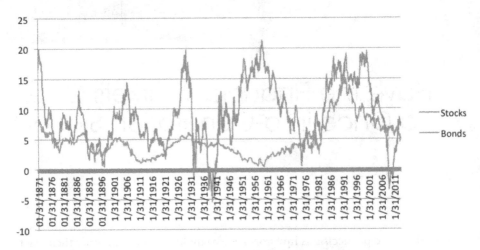

Figure 26.1 Ten-Year Total Returns to Stocks and Bonds, 1871 to 2011.

Global Financial Data has over 150 years of history on the interaction between the 10-year and 20-year returns on stocks and bonds in the United States. This amount of data provides a more realistic view of the information investors need to make long-term investment decisions. The 10-year total returns to stocks and bonds are illustrated in Figure 26.1.

Figure 26.1 illustrates that stocks generally outperform bonds over time, and that stock returns are more volatile than bond returns. What is more interesting than these well-known facts are the periodic, but rare, occasions when bonds outperform stocks over a 10-year period. The primary periods when stock returns fell below bond returns were in the 1880s and 1890s, the 1930s, the 1970s and the 2000s. Over the past 150 years, these have been once-in-a-generation events that are followed by periods of several decades in which stocks consistently outperform bonds, in some cases by wide margins.

Several important facts should be noted about this graph. In most cases, increases in the rate of return to stocks at the beginning of each cycle were accompanied by decreases in the rate of return to bonds, as was true from around 1900 to 1930 and from 1940 to 1970. This occurred when nominal interest rates were low at the beginning of a cycle.

The period between 1980 and 2005 was different from the other periods because the cycle began when inflation rates, and thus nominal interest rates, were relatively high. Consequently, as inflation and nominal interest rates fell, these changes generated capital gains which increased the long-term return to fixed income investors.

Once inflation fell to normal levels, the 10-year return on bonds began to fall. Yields on 10-year bonds have been declining consistently since 1981 which means that over the next few decades, the graph is more likely to look like the 1940s and

Figure 26.2 Twenty-Year Total Returns to Stocks and Bonds, 1871 to 2011.

1950s than the 1980s. It should also be noted that the 10-year relative returns to stocks and bonds cross over several times before stocks begin to consistently outperform bonds for a period of 25 years or more.

Although it is impossible to know the returns this graph will show over the next 30 years, stock returns will probably fluctuate dramatically over the rest of the decade. During the next bear market, whenever that may occur, 10-year returns to stocks will temporarily fall below the returns to bonds before rebounding. That will provide investors with a great opportunity to invest in stocks for the long run.

Figure 26.2 is the graph for the relative 20-year returns on stocks and bonds over the past 150 years. As can be seen, there have only been three times in the past 150 years when bond returns exceeded stock returns over a 20-year period: at the bottom of the bear market in 1932, at the beginning of the Bretton Woods era in 1949, and during during the financial crisis in 2009 and 2010. Since long-term bond total returns probably will continue to decline, 20-year stock returns are unlikely to drop below 20-year bond returns again for decades. As is true of the 10-year graph, stock and bond returns are beginning to diverge.

Although there is no guarantee financial markets will repeat their past performance, there are several possible implications of this once-in-a-lifetime signal from financial markets.

1. Stocks should generally outperform bonds over the next 30 years because a new cycle in the relative rates of return began in 2009.

2. When the current bull market runs into trouble sometime in the next few years, the relative 10-year return on stocks may temporarily fall below the return on bonds, but will soon recover.

3. The 10-year rate of return on bonds is in long-term decline, and is likely to continue. Because, unlike in the 1980s, inflation rates are not excessively high,

during the initial phase of this cycle, long-term return to bonds should decline not only in relative terms, but in absolute terms as well, before reversing about halfway through the cycle.

4. At the height of the cycle, stocks will have returned 15 percent–20 percent over the previous 10 years. This peak should be reached sometime in the 2020s.

5. This cycle reinforces the conclusions I made in my paper, "Are You Ready for the Bubble of the 2020s," which discusses the convergence of long-term factors which favor a strong bull market in the 2020s.

One possible conclusion to draw from these figures is that long-term investors should consider allocating more of their assets toward stocks, and take advantage of market downturns to reallocate money from bonds into stocks. Of course, past performance is no guarantee of future returns, but as anyone who looks at these graphs should realize, events such as these only happen once in a generation.

This leaves the question, if stocks are likely to outperform bonds over the next few decades and the "smart money" begins moving into stocks, who will be left to buy the bonds?

Of course, the Fed doesn't care about rates of return. They are buying bonds because this will supposedly have a beneficial effect on the economy. But if the "smart money" begins moving out of bonds and into stocks, what does this say about the Fed?

On the other hand, the Fed isn't using its own money to buy government bonds, but is creating it *ex nihilo* by expanding its spreadsheet. This means that the Fed not only is using "other people's money" to carry out policy, but it is using other people's money that previously did not exist.

Marty Zweig used to say, don't fight the Fed. This means that investors should not go short the market when the Fed is easing, or go long the market when the Fed is tightening. When the Fed simply influenced the economy by manipulating short-term interest rates, the Fed had no "skin in the game" whereby they could be adversely affected by their own decisions.

The Fed's transition to quantitative easing in which the Fed owns a substantial portion of any new debt issued by the Federal government means the Fed does have "skin in the game." Perhaps the chairman of the Fed should look at Figure 26.2 and reconsider the Fed's position.

chapter twenty-seven

Expansionism: The Impact of the Fed's Monetary Regime on Asset Class Returns

Investors allocate their assets into different classes both to reduce risk through portfolio diversification and to increase returns by changing these allocations. Financial assets have traditionally been divided into stocks, bonds and bills; non-traditional assets include housing, commodities, collectibles and other investments.

One of the primary questions the asset allocation process has raised is, what is the value of the Equity Risk Premium (ERP) as measured by the relative returns to equities against a risk-free investment, such as treasury bills in the short run and government bonds in the long run?

Risk and return are positively correlated. Equities are riskier than bonds and bills and should provide a higher rate of return to compensate investors for this risk. Over long periods of time, this has been true. Although risk is relative, the risk continuum starts at government T-Bills ("cash") and moves to government notes and bonds, corporate bonds, preferred stocks and to common stocks. The equity risk premium measures how much extra return investors should receive for the additional risk of moving up this risk continuum.

Most research has focused on determining the value of the ERP assuming it is a constant that could be directly related to the level of increased risk. Estimates of the equity risk premium are generally in the range of 3 to 7 percent depending upon the time period covered. However, the relative risk of stocks and bonds, as well as the perception of this risk changes over time. It is not fixed.

There is no agreement on the value of the ERP, primarily because historical comparisons of relative returns between stocks, bonds and bills vary greatly over time as well as between countries. In some cases, as in Japan between 1989 and 2013, the total return to government bonds has exceeded the return to equities over a period of 20 years or more. So if the ERP is not constant, why does it change over time, or does it even exist?

It is the argument of this chapter that a fixed value for the ERP may not even exist for two reasons. First, it is not possible to arbitrage the ERP, even when it significantly deviates from its long-term average. There is no historical evidence that it is possible to go long one asset class and short the other and profit from this arbitrage. The evidence for this is that the ERP can significantly differ from its long-term average for decades at a time. If the ERP could be arbitraged, such profitable opportunities would be eliminated more quickly than they are. The example of Japan in which the ERP was 10.07 between 1950 and 1989 and -4.79 from 1990 to 2016 is the best example of this.

The primary reason for this result is that equity returns are primarily driven by the growth in corporate profits, and nominal bond yields are driven by both inflation and the growth in the economy as a whole. Moreover, the business cycle driving equities is substantially shorter than the policy cycle driving bond yields. While a bull or bear market in equities may last two to five years, a bull or bear market in fixed income can last two or three decades. A fixed ERP assumes it is exogenous when in fact it may be endogenous and influenced by monetary and fiscal policy.

There is no fixed value for the Equity Risk Premium because both monetary and fiscal policy heavily influence the ERP over periods of a decade or less, primarily through the influence of monetary policy on fixed income returns, but also through the effect on equities. Expansionary fiscal policy only has a short-run impact on GDP. Fiscal policy influences the ERP by generating deficits because of wars, economic and financial crises, or other factors which influence the economy. Monetary policy is used to redress the problems created by government deficits and economic and financial crises, and impacts the money supply, inflation and interest rates, and thus the ERP.

Changes in interest rates produce a wealth effect through changes in bond prices and an income effect through changes in yields. Falling interest rates, as in the United States between 1981 and 2014 benefit fixed income investors through capital gains, but rising interest rates create capital losses. In extreme cases, government policies can completely wipe out an asset class, as happened with German Bonds in the 1920s. Hyperinflation can destroy the value of fixed income investments, or a currency change can wipe out savers by forcing them to convert to a new currency at an unfavorable rate, as happened in Germany in the 1940s. Monetary policy can and has negatively impacted investors, not only creating redistributions, but distorting returns to equities and to fixed income.

This chapter argues that different monetary regimes have existed over the past 150 years in the United States that have distorted bond and equity returns and influenced the equity risk premium in different ways. Although fiscal and monetary policies can also distort and influence the price of and return on housing, commodities and other asset classes, these effects will not be addressed here. The analysis will be limited to purely financial assets.

There are two implications of this. At the micro level, investors should adjust the allocation of their portfolios to reflect the impact of monetary policy on asset class returns. At the macro level, different monetary regimes not only influence the ERP, but they create distributional and economic inefficiencies that impact not only investors, but the economy as a whole. Most monetary policy fails to recognize this, concentrating on the need to encourage investment and consumption through manipulating interest rates or the money supply in order to influence GDP and unemployment, while ignoring the impact on asset returns to investors. Distortions to the ERP may last for decades. The full distributional and efficiency costs of these monetary regimes are usually ignored.

Monetary Regimes

A monetary regime is the general set of policies the government establishes toward the monetary side of the economy. The monetary regime can be based upon a gold standard or a fiat currency, on fixed or variable exchanges rates, on manipulating short-term and/or long-term interest rates, on controlling inflation or attempting to reduce unemployment, on manipulating reserves or the money supply, etc., or leaving these choices to the market.

The combination of policy choices that are made determines the monetary regime. As long as economic conditions remain favorable, providing economic growth, low unemployment and limited inflation, the monetary regime continues. If the economy falls into a recession or depression, a financial crisis can occur. When the existing monetary regime is no longer seen as a solution to the economy's problems, the monetary regime will change. Monetary regimes can also change in response to exogenous events, especially wars.

This chapter assumes the United States has gone through seven monetary regimes during the past 150 years, and entered into an eighth monetary regime in 2008. Economic crises within each monetary regime led to dissatisfaction with monetary policy leading to the introduction of a new monetary regime. These monetary regimes are outlined below.

Free Banking (1836–1861, Crisis in 1857)

The charter for the Second Bank of the United States expired in 1836. Between 1836 and 1913, the United States had no central bank, and until 1861, private banks were free to issue their own currency. The Panic of 1857 was the first worldwide financial crisis. Though the economy largely recovered by 1859, the end of free banking occurred more due to the Civil War than as a solution to the Panic of 1857.

Greenback Era (1861–1873, Crisis in 1869)

During the Civil War, the era of Free Banking was replaced by the Greenback Era when paper currency was not convertible into gold. Although many feared a debasement of the currency similar to what happened during the Revolutionary War, the Federal Government eventually returned to the gold standard, though this was not the case with the Confederacy where investors lost everything. The principle crisis of this era was Black Friday in 1869 when Jay Gould and others tried unsuccessfully to corner the gold market.

Gold Standard (1873–1913, Crisis in 1907)

The U.S. *de facto* returned to the gold standard in 1873 after the "Crime of 1873." The dollar was convertible into Gold during these years, but the Financial Crisis of 1907 led to the demand for a central bank that could offset the power of J. Pierpont Morgan and other private bankers. The Federal Reserve was created in 1913.

Federal Reserve Era (1913–1933, Crisis in 1929)

It was not the creation of the Fed, but World War I that determined the fate of the global economy during those 20 years. World War I created excessive debt throughout the world. The resulting imbalances made a return to the pre-war gold standard virtually impossible. Countries were unable to resolve the dislocations created by the debt and inflation created by the war. Attempts to return to a gold standard and seek international solutions failed, leading to the Great Depression.

War Economy (1933–1951, Post-War Inflation)

Because of the lack of an international consensus, each country sought different solutions to the Great Depression, primarily through expanding the role of government. Under Roosevelt, monetary policy was made subservient to fiscal policy and interest rates were controlled as government debt exploded. This led to higher inflation in the United States after the war, and to the Treasury Accord of 1951 which allowed the market to once again determine long-term interest rates.

Keynesianism (1951–1979, Stagflation in the 1970s)

Expansionary, countercyclical fiscal policy was seen as a way of reducing the fluctuations in the business cycle and creating growth, but excessive monetary expansion combined with the problems of the OPEC crisis, led to stagflation and rising interest rates. This led to dissatisfaction with Keynesianism and attempts to control inflation through monetary policy.

Bubblism (1979–2008, Great Recession of 2008)

Before 1979, the Fed generally targeted bank reserves in the financial system by setting the Fed Funds Rate. In October 1979, Volcker changed this policy to targeting the quantity of money, specifically, non-borrowed reserves; however, primarily due to financial innovations, the Fed's ability to control non-borrowed reserves and thus the money supply was limited. In October 1982, the Fed once again targeted interest rates rather than the quantity of money. This monetary regime is referred to as Bubblism because the accommodating monetary policies of the Fed after 1982 (the "Greenspan put") led to a series of financial bubbles and crises. Although Volcker's original Monetarist policies of 1979 drove down inflation by allowing interest rates to seek their own level, under Greenspan and Bernanke, low interest rates were used to offset financial recessions and crises including the 1987 Stock Market Crash, the S&L crisis, the Internet Bubble, and 9/11.

Expansionism (2008–)

After the financial crisis of 2008, short-term interest rates were driven down through the Fed's Zero Interest Rate Policy, while quantitative easing and other policies manipulated long-term interest rates. The Fed committed itself to expanding its balance sheet by buying government and mortgage-backed securities while the federal government ran trillion-dollar deficits after 2008.

Breaking up the past 150 years into these eight monetary regimes is meant to reflect the spirit of each era. Each of them could be broken down into shorter periods when additional policy changes occurred. Moreover, each regime was marked by a significant financial crisis leading to a major change in monetary policy. During these financial crises, returns to financial assets were below average while the economy suffered slow growth and/or inflation. As will be seen below, asset class returns differed significantly under each of these regimes, bringing into question the idea of a constant equity risk premium.

Although fiscal and monetary policy measures are usually framed primarily in terms of how they impact the economy as a whole, these policies also have substantial impacts on returns to investors. Monetary policy that impacts interest rates changes not only the returns to fixed-income investors, but impacts the ERP and consequently, the allocation of resources and economic efficiency. If individuals who are saving and investing for their retirement receive lower returns, their wealth and income are impacted.

Falling interest rates increase the wealth of fixed income investors through capital gains, but it reduces income from their wealth. Those who invest in bonds after interest rates fall are hurt by low returns, and do not benefit from the wealth effect. Similarly, when interest rates rise, there is a negative wealth effect, but a positive income effect. Monetary policy not only redistributes wealth and income through inflation and low interest rates, but impacts the allocation of resources and economic efficiency as well. Changes in the monetary regime create uncertainty as well as wealth and income effects.

The ideal monetary regime is one that allows the real side of the economy to allocate resources as efficiently as possible while minimizing the economic cost of the monetary side of the economy to the real economy. Ideally for investors, monetary regimes should change as little as possible. In reality, although central banks may have *de jure* independence, in practice their policies must accommodate politically-motivated fiscal policy, and consider both the political and economic trade-offs of accommodative monetary policy.

This chapter argues that the equity risk premium not only measures the relative returns of stocks, bonds and bills, but it also measures the endogenous distortions to the financial sector created by monetary and fiscal policy. Unfortunately, there are few opportunities to arbitrage these distortions successfully. Fluctuations in the ERP are a measure of the redistributions and inefficiencies created by monetary and fiscal policy. These distortions misallocate resources and may contribute to the severity of the financial and economic crises that occur.

Asset Class Returns in Theory

The returns to stocks, bonds and bills depend upon different factors. Bills are cash instruments that provide return with no risk. They should compensate the investor for inflation, and their rate of return should equal the inflation rate in the long run with some allowance for the time value of money. The return on default-risk-free government bonds should equal the growth in nominal GDP since this is the opportunity cost of money over long periods of time. The return on corporate equities should depend on the growth in future corporate profits, allowing for the riskiness of the company and its securities. The value of a company, and thus its stock, is the risk-adjusted present value of future cash flows to investors. Utility stocks provide different returns than do biotech companies, and corporate bonds, preferred stocks and common stocks all have different returns because of the risk of receiving the firm's future cash flows.

The optimal monetary regime is one that minimizes the cost to the real economy of the financial system. The Fed's directive is to control inflation while maintaining growth and minimizing unemployment. These goals cannot be achieved simultaneously, so the Fed must look at the trade-offs between controlling inflation and increasing economic output. Similarly, the Fed needs to consider the impact of its policies on the allocation of financial resources, the wealth and income effects that occur for investors and savers, and how the Fed's choices may lead to a financial crisis which imposes costs on the economy.

Monetary regimes impact inflation and thus the returns to bills. Investors try to predict future inflation rates, economic growth rates and future profits, and reallocate investments to reflect their expectations. Similarly, investors attempt to predict the present value of future cash flows to different corporations and change their investments in equities accordingly.

If fixed-income investors underestimate future inflation, as occurred in the 1970s, they receive negative returns. If the government artificially lowers interest rates, as in the 1940s and 2010s, bondholders have less income. Similarly, unwarranted expectations of economic growth, fueled by low interest rates or an expansive monetary regime, can lead to an expansion in the PE ratio for equities (as in the 1960s and 1990s), leading to excessive returns to shareholders in one decade, which can lead to a reversion to the mean, and thus lower returns, in the decade that follows.

Different fundamental factors drive returns to equities and fixed income. Equity returns are primarily driven by GDP growth and nominal fixed income returns by inflation. Fiscal and monetary policy also impact returns to both assets in different ways, and different factors drive the wealth and income effects on returns to both.

For these reasons, the time cycles of bull and bear markets in equities and fixed income differ, and this combination of factors makes it very difficult to arbitrage deviations from the average ERP, even when this persists for a decade or more. Consequently, it is important that investors understand how the existing monetary regime impacts returns to equities and fixed income and the distortions and misallocations the existing monetary regime creates.

Asset Class Returns under Different Monetary Regimes

It is the argument of this chapter that the monetary regime chosen by the government influences the relative returns to different asset classes. Table 27.1 illustrates this.

Table 27.1 Annual Nominal Asset Class Returns under Different Monetary Regimes

Regime	Years	S&P 500	Bonds	Portfolio	Bills	Inflation	CHF	GDP
Greenback	1861–1873	15.41	7.5	11.46	4.89	2.82	–0.05	3.3
Gold Standard	1874–1913	6.16	3.34	4.75	2.95	0.44	0.04	3.31
Federal Reserve	1914–1932	4.99	4.21	4.60	3.35	1.43	–0.02	0.74
War Economics	1933–1950	12.15	3.03	7.59	0.42	3.66	–1.05	5.97
Keynesianism	1951–1979	10.15	3.2	6.68	4.27	3.94	–3.36	3.69
Bubblism	1980–2008	10.72	9.8	10.26	5.77	3.54	–1.38	2.83
Expansionism	2009–2016	14.45	1.54	7.99	0.11	1.74	–1.10	1.75
Pre-Federal Reserve	1871–1913	6.23	3.65	4.94	3.08	0.32	0.04	4.72
Federal Reserve Era	1914–2016	9.99	5.15	7.57	3.54	3.15	–1.60	3.15
All	1871–2016	8.88	4.63	6.77	3.38	2.30	–1.10	3.61

Table 27.1 shows the returns to stocks, bonds and bills during each of the Monetary Regimes discussed above. Although the Greenback Era is included, reliable dividend data are only available since 1871. The Portfolio consists of 50 percent Bonds and 50 percent Equities. Summary numbers for returns before the Federal Reserve in 1913, after 1913 and the entire period from 1871 to 2016 are also provided.

The first table shows nominal returns to different asset classes as well as GDP growth during each period and the change in the U.S. against the Swiss Franc which has been the strongest global currency over the past 100 years. The table clearly shows differences in the returns to stocks, bonds and bills under the different monetary regimes.

Table 27.2 shows real returns to different asset classes as well as the Equity/Government Bond Risk Premium, GDP and per capita GDP.

Two questions are paramount here: 1) Have the monetary regimes impacted the returns to different asset classes? 2) Have these returns differed under the Federal Reserve and the era before the creation of the Fed? The bar chart in Figure 27.1 shows clear differences in the returns under different monetary regimes.

As the data reveal in Figure 27.2, returns to stocks, bonds and bills have varied substantially from one monetary regime to the other as has the equity/bond premium. The data substantiate the basic premise of this chapter that monetary regimes influence investment returns. Real equity returns ranged from 3.51 percent

Table 27.2 Annual Real Asset Class Returns under Different Monetary Regimes

Regime	Years	Stocks	Bonds	Portfolio	Bills	ERP	GDP	Per Capita
Greenback	1861–1873	12.24	4.55	8.39	2	7.35	3.3	0.84
Gold Standard	1874–1913	5.70	2.89	4.29	2.5	2.73	3.31	0.88
Federal Reserve	1914–1932	3.51	2.74	3.13	1.9	0.75	0.74	–0.59
War Economics	1933–1950	8.19	–0.61	3.79	–3.12	8.85	5.97	4.61
Keynesianism	1951–1979	5.97	–0.71	2.63	0.32	6.73	3.69	2.32
Bubblism	1980–2008	6.93	6.05	6.49	2.15	0.83	2.83	1.74
Expansionism	2009–2016	12.45	–0.21	6.14	–1.60	12.72	1.75	0.95
Pre-Federal Reserve	1871–1913	5.89	3.32	4.6	2.75	2.49	4.72	2.57
Federal Reserve	1914–2016	6.63	1.94	4.29	0.38	4.60	3.15	2.03
All	1871–2016	6.43	2.28	4.36	1.05	4.06	3.61	2.19

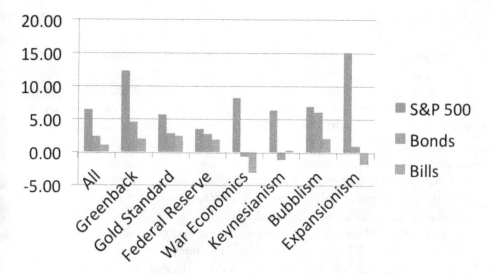

Figure 27.1 Real Returns to Stocks Bonds and Bills Under Different Monetary Regimes.

per annum in 1914–1932 to 12.45 percent in 2008–2016 (ignoring the Greenback Era). Bond returns ranged from –0.71 percent under the Keynesian regime to 6.05 percent under Bubblism. While the Equity/Bond Premium averaged over 8 percent between 1933 and 1981, in part because real returns to government bonds were negative, it was only 0.83 percent between 1980 and 2008.

Comparing the periods before and after the creation of the Federal Reserve shows that GDP growth was higher, on average, before the creation of the Federal Reserve, though real equity returns were higher after 1913. Although there are many other factors influencing Real GDP Per Capita growth than the Federal Reserve, the data make it hard to argue that activist monetary and fiscal policy are required for long-term economic growth.

The primary impact of Federal Reserve policies can be seen in the returns to bonds and bills, as well as the impact on the exchange rate. Returns to bondholders have been both lower and more volatile since the creation of the Federal Reserve than before. Bondholders received negative real returns between 1933 and 1979 as interest rates rose, but made substantially higher returns after 1980 as monetary policies pushed down interest rates. The real yield on T-bills also fell substantially under the Federal Reserve. This increased the annual Equity/Bond Premium from 2.49 percent before 1914 to 4.60 percent after 1913. However, this ERP fell to 0.83 percent between 1980 and 2008. A critic of the Fed might point out that Monetary Policy under the Fed has increased the volatility of returns to investors, distorting the allocation of resources without increasing returns.

The average inflation rate before 1914 was 0.32 percent, but 3.17 percent after 1913. Although there was virtually no change in the exchange rate between the USD and the Swiss franc before the Federal Reserve was founded, the USD has depreciated at an annual rate of 1.63 percent per annum against the Swiss franc since the Federal Reserve was created to defend the U.S. dollar.

The goal of activist monetary and fiscal policy in the United States is to maintain growth, limit unemployment and control inflation. There are arguments as to how well the Fed has succeeded in achieving these goals, but the tables show that returns to investors have also been impacted by the different monetary regimes that have existed since 1913. Policy discussions usually focus on the impact of fiscal and monetary policy on GDP, unemployment and inflation, but ignore the impact on investors which is illustrated above.

One could argue that fixed-income investors have borne most of the "cost" of activist government policies, not only in actual returns, but in the variability of those returns, which has increased since the creation of the Federal Reserve. Although it would seem that the creation of the Fed would benefit fixed-income investors and the USD since the Fed would attempt to reduce the volatility of the market, in fact, they have been the Fed's victims. The misallocations and transfers caused by these policies are often ignored in the formulation of economic policy, but these costs do exist.

An Overview of the Monetary Regimes

The Greenback Era was marked by inflation during the Civil War and deflation after the war so the United States could eliminate the Gold Premium relative to paper dollars. The low inflation rate over this period masks the rise and fall in prices that occurred between 1861 and 1873. People remembered that the Continental Congress had defaulted on its obligations and created inflation making paper money almost worthless. Although the Federal government returned to the gold standard after the Civil War, the Confederacy defaulted on its obligations wiping out holders of Confederate financial assets.

The strong returns to stocks and bonds during the Greenback Era reflect, in part, the fact that the stock market was at a low point when the war began and bond yields had peaked. The stock market rose continually during the war, peaking in 1873 while bond yields fell from 1861 until the early 1900s (Figure 27.2). This pattern continued during the Gold Standard Regime with strong bull markets occurring between 1876 and 1881 and between 1896 and 1901. Stocks fluctuated within ranges during the rest of the period between 1878 and 1913. Despite the sharp break in 1907, the market immediately bounced back. The most notable fact about the period before 1913 was the stability of prices, the currency and of government spending, and the relative stability of the Equity Risk Premium.

Although the Federal Reserve was created in 1913, the more important event was the start of World War I in 1914. The result in the U.S. was double-digit inflation from 1916 to 1919 and deflation through 1932. The inflation during and

Price ■ USA 10-year Bond Constant Maturity Yield (IGUSA10D)

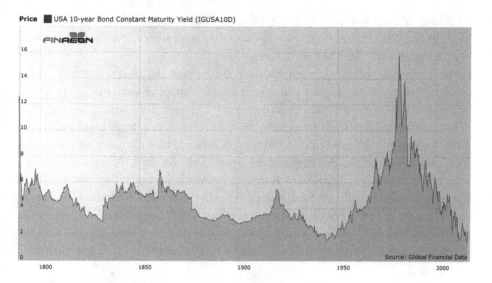

Figure 27.2 Yield on the U.S. 10-year Bond 1790 to 2014.

after the war created wild fluctuations for investors with strong losses until 1921, a huge bull market through 1929 and a sharp crash to 1932. Bond yields rose through 1921, then declined steadily until the 1940s.

The creation of the Fed coincided with the collapse of the Pound Standard, often referred to as the Gold Standard, after World War I. Britain was unable to bear the burden of the financial and economic costs of World War I, and was unable to return to their old gold parity in the 1920s. Financial and economic conditions in other countries were even worse than in Britain with hyperinflation wiping out German investors. The inability or unwillingness of the United States to replace the Pound Standard with a Dollar Standard until Bretton Woods contributed to the economic problems of the 1930s.

The volatility of this period had more to do with the war and the fiscal policy resulting from the war and its consequences than with monetary policy. The inability of both American and European politicians to successfully deal with the financial and economic problems that resulted from World War I have a parallel in the inability of American and European politicians to successfully deal with the current economic crisis. It is difficult to get society to bear the costs of addressing a financial crisis when the economy is in a recession or suffering slow growth with high unemployment.

Even after Roosevelt was elected in 1933 and fiscal policy became paramount, stock market declines in 1937 and 1941 returned the market to the level it had been at in 1901. Once the war began, the U.S. government made sure it didn't suffer the inflation of World War I by controlling prices, interest rates and spending. The stock market boomed during the war, paused during the post-war recession, then rose almost continually from 1948 to 1966. Interest rates were kept low throughout World War II, and even though they were allowed to rise after the war, they remained low until the early 1960s.

Nevertheless, inflation gradually rose throughout the post-war era, pushing nominal interest rates higher and creating a slow-moving bear market in bonds that lasted until interest rates peaked in 1981. Between 1966 and 1981, the S&P 500 lost almost 75 percent of its value in real terms as long-term bond yields rose from 5 percent to 15 percent. With stocks, bonds and bills all suffering real losses, Volcker introduced policies designed to control inflation in 1979, even if it caused a recession. However, because of financial innovation, controlling the monetary aggregates proved difficult and monetary policy switched back to focusing on interest rates in 1982. For interest rates, the 1981–2017 period was a mirror image of the 1951 to 1981 period with interest rates making a round trip back to the levels of less than 2 percent that occurred during World War II. This is illustrated in Figure 27.2.

There is a certain irony in that the solutions that were laid down at the beginning of each monetary regime, and initially appeared to succeed, ultimately failed. The return to gold in 1873 ultimately led to the creation of the Fed which led to a fiat currency replacing gold. The financial crisis of 1907 which gave rise to the creation of the Fed led to a collapse in the money supply in the 1930s, contributing to the Great Depression. The government's control over interest rates and bond yields in the 1940s led to the Treasury Accord which allowed the market to determine long-term interest rates and eventually led to the highest interest rates in U.S. history.

The failure of Keynesian policies in the 1970s led to the introduction of Monetarist policies in 1979, interest rate targeting after 1982, and the Bubblism of the 1990s and 2000s. Although price inflation declined, asset inflation became a significant problem. Volcker allowed interest rates to seek their own level to control inflation, but Greenspan and Bernanke drove interest rates down to unprecedented levels to save the economy. Government deficits worsened creating further pressure on monetary policy.

In 2008, the worst economic crisis since the Great Depression occurred. Despite fiscal stimulus through trillion-dollar government deficits, and monetary stimulus through QE1, QE2, Operation Twist, expansion of the Fed's balance sheet, large purchases of government debt, and other measures, strong growth failed to return. To prevent the economy from falling into a deep recession, the government ran trillion-dollar deficits for several years, and the Fed expanded its balance sheet to over $3 trillion by purchasing U.S. government and mortgage-backed securities. This constitutes a new monetary regime, which we refer to as expansionism because of the expansion in government spending, in the government deficit, and in the Fed's Balance Sheet. At this point, one can only wonder what financial crisis expansionism is creating for the 2020s or 2030s.

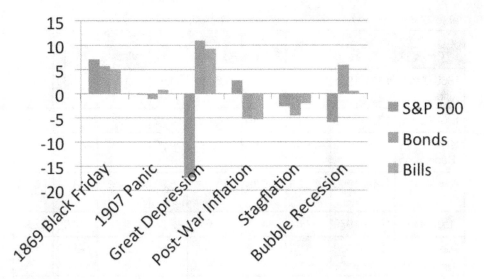

Figure 27.3 Real Returns to Stocks, Bonds and Bills During Monetary Regime Crises.

Returns during Crisis Periods at the End of Monetary Regimes

Since each monetary regime covers long periods of time, the data can mask the large swings and returns that occur within each monetary regime (Figure 27.3). The change from the gold standard to the creation of a central bank, from 1930s deflation to Keynesian inflation, from the emphasis on Keynesian fiscal policy to monetary policy occurred because existing monetary regimes failed to provide growth to the economy at low inflation rates. It will be shown here that during each crisis period, investors suffered substantially, contributing to the demand for a change in monetary regimes.

Although we are focusing on monetary regimes, it remains true that fiscal policy influences GDP growth and returns as well. Fiscal and monetary policy do not exist in a vacuum. Each of the crises at the end of each monetary regime was influenced by outside "real world" events which monetary policy could only react to.

The important point to recognize here is that during each crisis, the existing monetary regime was no longer able to solve the problems that existed. Whether each monetary regime laid the seeds of its own destruction, or if the results would have been different under a different monetary regime is difficult to determine. Nevertheless, the crisis created a need for a "solution" to the existing economic problems and a change in monetary regimes.

Table 27.3 shows that returns to investors at the end of each monetary regime were substantially lower than the average for each period. Either equities or bonds provided negative returns during each of these crises save one. In four of

189

Table 27.3 Annual Real Asset Class Returns during Different Financial Crises

Crisis	Years	S&P 500	Bonds	Portfolio	Bills	Inflation	ERP	GDP
1869 Black Friday	1869–1873	7.08	5.69	6.38	4.93	−1.53	1.32	4.4
1907 Panic	1907–1913	−0.28	−1.10	−0.69	0.72	2.30	0.83	2.91
1929 Depression	1929–1932	−17.47	10.90	−3.29	9.22	−6.44	−25.58	−5.69
Post-War Inflation	1946–1950	2.65	−5.19	−1.27	−5.33	6.55	8.27	0.48
Stagflation	1973–1979	−2.64	−4.58	−3.61	−2.06	8.82	2.03	2.93
Bubble Recession	2000–2008	−5.96	5.94	−0.01	0.52	2.50	−1.23	1.76

the six periods, a portfolio invested half in equities and half in bonds generated negative returns during each crisis except for the Great Recession and the Black Friday Panic.

Given this data, it is easy to see why there was dissatisfaction with the existing monetary regime and a demand for change. Each crisis led to an important change in monetary policy that set the tone for the next few decades: returning to a *de facto* gold standard in 1873, creating the Federal Reserve in 1913, subordinating monetary policy to fiscal policy after the election of Roosevelt in 1933, allowing the market to set government bond yields after 1951, controlling inflation through activist monetary policy after 1979, and the combination of a zero interest rate policy and quantitative easing after 2008.

Although the Great Recession provided high returns to fixed income, this was offset by the negative returns to equities. The severity of the Great Recession of 2008 produced a significant change in monetary policy, lowering interest rates to zero and using the Fed's Balance Sheet as an important tool to combat slow growth. For this reason, we consider these policies a regime change within our paradigm.

The Case of Japan

The United States remains mired in a period of slow growth and low job creation despite the activist monetary and fiscal policy that has occurred since 2008. Under the new monetary regime of expansionism, the U.S. government has run trillion-dollar annual deficits, dramatically increased the money supply and expanded the Fed's Balance Sheet, while pushing both short-run and long-run interest rates down to unprecedented levels.

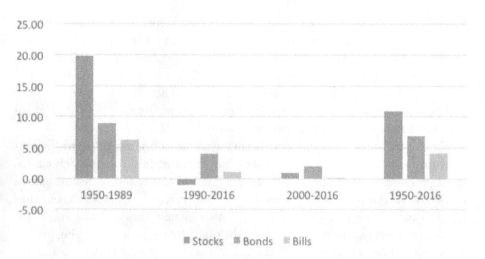

Figure 27.4 Real Returns to Stocks, Bonds and Bills in Japan 1950 to 2016.

These policies are very similar to the ones Japan has followed for the past two decades, so it is important to look at the impact these policies have had on investors in Japan. If the United States is following monetary policies similar to the ones Japan has followed, similar results may occur.

Since 1990, Japan has suffered low growth and provided low or negative returns to investors. Japan's nominal GDP remains virtually unchanged since 1990 and the Japanese stock market in 2017 is at the same price levels it was at in 1986. Japanese interest rates have been the lowest in the world (the 10-year bond currently yields less than 1 percent) during the past 20 years, and Japan has had no inflation since 1990. Figure 27.4 illustrates the impact of this slow growth on Japanese investors.

Table 27.4 shows the returns to stocks, bonds and bills in Japan since 1950. The table reinforces the fact that the Equity Risk Premium can change dramatically. Between 1950 and 1989 when Japan was growing and went through its bubble in the 1980s, the Stock/Bond Premium averaged 10.41 percent per annum over a period of almost 40 years, but since 1989, equity returns have been negative, and the ERP has been –5.49 percent. Housing prices remain substantially below the

Table 27.4 Japan Real Asset Returns during Different Time Periods

Years	Stocks	Bonds	Bills	Portfolio	ERP	Inflation	Real GDP
1950–1989	14.11	3.67	1.13	8.89	10.07	5.01	7.19
1990–2016	–1.46	3.5	0.67	1.02	–4.79	0.41	0.65
2000–2016	0.81	1.94	0.11	1.37	–1.41	0.08	0.31
1950–2016	7.56	3.6	0.94	5.58	–3.82	3.13	4.56

levels they were at in 1989 as well. The average annual return to bonds and bills has been relatively consistent, but the return on equities has varied considerably. Japan's lost two decades have generated negative returns for shareholders for over 25 years.

Unfortunately, there are substantial parallels between Japan in the 1990s and the United States in the 2010s. Despite nine years of activist fiscal and monetary policy, economic growth remains slow. Continuous government deficits in Japan have not resulted in a return to economic growth.

Current Fed policy has followed Japan's example in driving long-term interest rates to unprecedented lows. This policy has benefited investors through capital gains on bonds which increase wealth, but this will reduce future income earned on bonds. This creates a dilemma for fixed-income investors similar to the one they faced in the United States in the 1940s. Either interest rates stay low and fixed-income investors receive low returns over their investment horizon, or rising interest rates trap them in a bear market that reduces wealth. Anyone saving for retirement or other future goals will find it difficult to obtain adequate returns from bonds. The equity risk premium can rise by default through low returns to fixed income, but the negative returns to shareholders in Japan during the past 20 years has meant that despite low bond yields, fixed income has outperformed equities.

The greatest fear is that as in Japan, the United States suffers two decades of inferior economic growth, slow job growth, low interest rates which negatively impact investors, and low equity returns. The United States has already lost one decade of growth during the 2000s despite massively accommodating fiscal and monetary policy. Is it doomed to a second lost decade?

The Fed's Four Failures

Just as the nineteenth century was dominated by the Pound Standard with currencies linked to gold, the twentieth century was dominated by the Dollar Standard with fiat currencies controlled by central banks. Before World War I, many countries still allowed private banks to print banknotes, but by World War II, this privilege had been almost completely withdrawn.

In 2013, the Federal Reserve marked its hundredth anniversary, but it was a century in which the Fed failed four times.

The first failure occurred in the 1930s when the Fed allowed the money supply to collapse, contributing to the severity of the Great Depression in the United States. This was compounded by the inability and unwillingness of the United States to step in as the primary central bank in the global financial system after the United Kingdom failed to maintain its role after it failed to return to the pre-war exchange rate parity in the 1920s. The Fed failed both domestically and internationally, making the Great Depression worse than it might have otherwise been.

The second failure occurred in the 1970s when the Fed failed to contain the inflation that built up through increases in the money supply. This led to the highest inflation rates in U.S. history, outside of the Revolutionary and Civil Wars, and the highest interest rates in U.S. history. Paul Volcker had to dramatically change Fed policy in order to defeat the inflation that appeared to have become endemic in the American economy.

The third failure occurred in the 2000s, when the Greenspan put finally failed. The Bubblism of the 1990s and 2000s led to the Great Recession of 2008 and a new monetary regime of expansionism. The failure to contain asset price bubbles, and the consequences that they created for the economy, contributed to the magnitude of the financial collapse when it occurred. The collapse of the housing market after 2006 created problems which could take a decade to undo.

The fourth failure has been the cost to investors over the long run of Fed policies. As illustrated in this chapter, the manipulation of interest rates, directly on short-term interest rates through control of the Fed Funds rate and the discount rate, or on long-term bonds through quantitative easing, or indirectly through higher interest rates caused by higher inflation, has imposed costs on investors. Both interest rates themselves, as well as the Equity Risk Premium, have been more volatile since the creation of the Fed than they were before 1913. Similarly, the Fed has allowed the U.S. dollar to depreciate dramatically against the Swiss franc, Deutsche Mark/Euro and other currencies, also imposing costs on U.S. investors as well as on foreigners who hold American financial assets.

The fourth failure, though perhaps the least recognized of the four, has also had high economic costs and has created redistributions of income and wealth over time. The Fed is required by law to both control inflation and promote economic growth, and has done so primarily through the manipulation of short-term interest rates. But this policy has come at an often unrecognized cost to investors through the wealth effects caused by rising and falling interest rates and thus bond prices, through the income effect resulting from changing interest rates, from the uncertainty caused by the changes in interest rates, through the impact this has had on the Equity Risk Premium, and through the redistributions and distortions caused by the mispricing of financial assets caused by the Fed's intervention.

How Will Expansionism Impact Investors?

Expansionism describes the current fiscal and monetary policy that the United States has pursued since 2008. It is a combination of massive stimulus from fiscal policy, combined with various types of quantitative easing and negative real interest rates through the Fed's interest rate policy. Monetary policy has accommodated fiscal policy through the expansion of the Fed's balance sheet, driving short-term interest rates close to zero and manipulating long-term interest rates through the purchase of Federal government bonds.

The potential problems with expansionism are several. First, these policies have yet to generate sustainable long-term economic growth. Second, the manipulation of interest rates creates redistributions of income and misallocations of resources that impose costs on the economy as a whole. Fixed income investors face low returns either through low interest rates or capital losses if high inflation raises nominal interest rates. Third, annual multi-billion dollar deficits raise the government debt/GDP ratio. The current government debt/GDP ratio is sustainable because of low interest rates, but should interest rates rise, the United States could run into problems as higher interest costs impact the federal budget.

The costs to the economy of expansionism in terms of rising government debt, low returns to investors and a declining dollar could at some point lead to an even worse financial crisis. At best, expansionism is a way of buying time until the economy recovers on its own, but if the economy fails to recover, these policies could lay the foundations of an even worse financial crisis during which the United States would be forced to deleverage its debt.

Deleveraging involves reducing the debt levels that have built up over time in order that a deeper financial crisis does not occur. Although deleveraging may be beneficial in the long-run, in the short-run it can reduce aggregate demand and GDP. The goal of deleveraging is to lower the debt/GDP ratio. This can be done either through fiscal policy via austerity measures, or through monetary policy via inflation.

Deleveraging through fiscal policy can occur either by running government budget surpluses or by running deficits that are lower than the rate of economic growth. The United Kingdom was able to reduce its Napoleonic War debt, and the United States its World War II debt without paying off their debts when their rates of GDP growth exceeded government deficits.

Failure to deleverage can lead to rioting by the financial markets. This can lead to higher yields on government debt and either default or reliance on international lenders who enforce austerity programs in exchange for the loans the private market is unwilling to provide.

Deleveraging can also occur through inflation, reducing the real debt burden by inflating out of it. France suffered constant financial crisis during the 1930s in part because of its high government debt/GDP ratio. After the war, its debt was substantially reduced by inflation (Germany used a currency conversion to reduce its debt after World War II and then renegotiated its existing international debts). Although investors paid a high price for the deleveraging, it did allow France to concentrate more of its resources on investment and growth after World War II.

Deleveraging through inflation imposes substantial costs on debt-holders, but it provides an alternative when political paralysis prevents the country from restructuring its fiscal policy to address the problems of rising government debt. Given the Federal government's inability to reduce its large budget deficits, the possibility that the United States government might deleverage through inflation should not be rejected. If this were to occur, fixed-income investors would suffer, while equities would increase in value as the nominal assets that underlie equities rose in value.

Conclusion

There are two conclusions to be drawn from the evidence presented above. First, investors cannot ignore the influence of monetary policy on the returns to stocks, bonds and bills, both in absolute and in relative terms. The differences in the returns to fixed-income securities between 1878 and 1933, 1933 and 1981 as well as 1981 and 2017 are best explained by changes in monetary policy that drove interest rates up from 1933 to 1981 and down from 1981 to 2017. These policies not only distorted returns to financial assets, but also created misallocations in the economy that may have contributed to the financial crises that occurred. Central bank policy has generally subordinated the impact of monetary policy on investor returns to economic policy goals such as stable-long run growth and low unemployment.

Second, the evidence here raises the question of whether the different monetary regimes that have existed in the past, even assuming that they have produced net benefits to the economy as a whole, have created distortions and misallocations whose costs to investors exceed their benefits. Since 2008, the Fed has pursued a policy of expansionism that has reduced short-term interest rates, and manipulated long-term interest rates through the purchase of government securities.

As stated earlier, the ideal monetary regime is one that allows the real side of the economy to allocate resources as efficiently as possible while minimizing the economic cost of the monetary side of the economy. The Fed has worked to achieve this goal by controlling inflation, but the other policy goals imposed upon or chosen by the Fed, to increase growth, reduce unemployment or absorb government debt impose real costs on the economy. The Fed has subjugated important goals on the monetary and financial side of the economy, such as controlling credit expansion, limiting asset bubbles, and the impact of monetary policy on returns to investors to achieving goals in the real economy which it may not be able to attain.

Expansionism is the current monetary regime of the United States. This regime could continue for several decades as it has in Japan, or as has occurred with other monetary regimes. Expansionism can, and probably will, sow the seeds of its own destruction, leading to another financial crisis at some point in the 2020s or 2030s.

Investors should be aware of the costs of monetary policy, not only in terms of the macroeconomic impact of monetary policy, but the impact on investor returns.

The current activist policies of the Fed continue to impose costs, reallocate and misallocate financial and real resources, just as previous monetary regimes have. The failure of Activist policies in Japan to provide high returns to investors over the past two decades is a cause for deep concern to investors in both the United States and in Europe where similar policies are being pursued.

Sources for Further Reading

Most articles used information from Wikipedia. Data for figures and tables are taken from the Global Financial Database. Sourcing for the data is provided in the Global Financial Database.

Historical information on the changing role of gold in the economy can be found in Pierre Vilar, *A History of Gold and Money*, London: NLB, 1969, William Arthur Shaw, *The History of Currency, 1252 to 1896*, New York: Augustus M. Kelley, 1967, Glyn Davies, *A History of Money*, Cardiff, Cardiff: University of Wales Press, 2002, and Jack Weatherford, *The History of Money*, New York: Crown Publishers, 1997. Information for more specific periods of time are covered in Peter Spufford, *Money and Its Use in Medieval Europe*, Cambridge: Cambridge University Press, 1988; Philip Grierson and Mark Blackburn, *Medieval European Coinage: The Early Middle Ages*, Cambridge: Cambridge University Press, 1986; Robert Chalmers, *A History of Currency in the British Colonies*, Ann Arbor: University of Michigan Library, 1893 and Nicholas Mayhew, *Sterling, The History of a Currency*, New York: John Wiley & Sons, Inc., 1999.

The classic article on hyperinflation is Philip Cagan, "The Monetary Dynamics of Hyperinflation," in Milton Friedman (Editor), *Studies in the Quantity Theory of Money*, Chicago: University of Chicago Press (1956). Hanke-Krus provides a list of 51 hyperinflations that fit Cagan's definition in Steve H. Hanke and Nicholas Krus, "World Hyperinflations" in Randall Parker and Robert Whaples (eds.), *The Handbook of Major Events in Economic History*, London: Routledge Publishing, 2013, pp. 367–377.

On the Hungarian hyperinflation, see W. A. Bomberger and G. E. Makinen, *"Indexation, Inflationary Finance, and Hyperinflation: The 1945–1946 Hungarian Experience"*. *Journal of Political Economy, 1980, 88 (3): 550–560*. On the Zimbabwe hyperinflation, see Steve H. Hanke, "Zimbabwe: From Hyperinflation to Growth," *Development Policy Analysis No. 6.*, Cato Institute, Center for Global Liberty and Prosperity. (June 25, 2008) and Philip Haslam and Russell Lamberti, *When Money Destroys Nations: How Hyperinflation Ruined Zimbabwe, How Ordinary People*

Survived, and Warnings for Nations that Print Money, Johannesburg: Penguin Books (South Africa), 2015. The currencies issued during the Hungarian inflation can be found in George S. Cuhaj, *Standard Catalog of World Paper Money*, Iola, WI: Krause Publications and the currencies issued in Yugoslavia and Zimbabwe can be found in George S. Cuhaj, *Standard Catalog of World Paper Money, 1961–Present*, Iola, WI: Krause Publications.

A good source on the German Currency reform is F. A. Lutz, "The German Currency Reform and the Revival of the German Economy," *Economica,* New Series, Vol. 16, No. 62 (May, 1949), pp. 122–142, Eckhard Wandel, "Historical Developments Prior to the German Currency Reform of 1948", *Zeitschrift für die gesamte Staatswissenschaft / Journal of Institutional and Theoretical Economics* Bd. 135, H. 3. (September 1979), pp. 320–331 and World Bank, *The currency reform in the Western zones of Germany—summary and conclusions.* Washington, DC: World Bank, 1948.

For information on the history of foreign exchange and historical exchange rates, see Peter Spufford, *Handbook of Medieval Exchange*, London: Offices of the Royal Historical Society, 1986, Paul Enzig, *The History of Foreign Exchange*, New York: St. Martin's Press, 1962, Markus A. Denzel, *Handbook of World Exchange Rates, 1590–1914*, Burlington: Ashgate Publishing Co, 2010, and Michael W. Klein and Jay C. Shambaugh, *Exchange Rate Regimes in the Modern Era*, Cambridge, MA: MIT Press, 2012.

Information on sovereign defaults in the two articles on Greece was obtained from Barry Eichengreen, "Settling Defaults in the Era of Bond Finance," *The World Bank Economic Review*, Vol. 3, No. 2, 21, 1–239, and Michael Tomz, *Reputation and International Cooperation: Sovereign Debt Across Three Centuries*, Princeton: Princeton University Press, 2007.

The classic book on interest rates is Sidney Homer and Richard Sylla, *A History of Interest Rates*, 4th Edition, New York: Wiley, 2005. This source was used for both "Seven Centuries of Government Bond Yields" and "Birds, Boats and Bonds in Venice: The First AAA Government Bond Issue." A long-term overview of financial crises can be found in Carmen M. Reinhart and Kenneth Rogoff, *This Time is Different: Eight Centuries of Financial Folly*, Princeton: Princeton University Press, 2011. For changes in the center of the financial world over time, see Charles P. Kindleberger, *A Financial History of Western Europe*, London, George Allen & Unwin, 1984 and Charles P. Kindleberger, *World Economic Primacy, 1500–1990*, Oxford: Oxford University Press, 1996.

Two books on the Greek debt crisis include Matthew Lynn, *Bust: Greece, the Euro and the Sovereign Debt Crisis*, Hoboken, N.J.: Bloomberg Press, 2010, and Jason Manolopoulos, *Greece's 'Odious' Debt: The Looting of the Hellenic Republic by the Euro, the Political Elite and the Investment Community*, New York: Anthem Press, 2011.

The story of Artur Alves Reis was originally recounted in Murray Teigh Bloom, *Money of their Own: The True Stories of the World's Greatest Counterfeiters*, New York: Scribner, 1957. Bloom then converted this story into a fascinating book, Murray Teigh Bloom, *The Man Who Stole Portugal*, New York: Scribner, 1966. See also Sir Cecil H. Kisch, *The Portuguese Bank Note Case*, London: MacMillan and Co., Ltd, 1932.

Much has been written on the German hyperinflation. Two useful, recent books are Frederick Taylor, *The Downfall of Money: Germany's Hyperinflation and the Destruction of the Middle Class*, New York: Bloomsbury Press, 2015 and Adam Fergusson, *When Money Dies: The Nightmare of Deficit Spending, Devaluation and Hyperinflation in Weimar Germany*, New York: Public Affairs, 2010.

For more information on Confederate Bonds, see George C. Criswell, Jr., *Confederate and Southern State Bonds*, Volume 2, Ft. McCoy, FL: Criswell's & Criswell's Publications, 1979. The near default of the United States in 1895 is retold in Jean Strouse, *Morgan: American Financier*, New York: Random House, 2014. See also Ron Chernow, *The House of Morgan: An American Banking Dynasty and the Rise of Modern Finance*, New York: Atlantic Monthly Press, 1990.

The Financial Crisis of 33 AD is covered in Otto Lightner, *The History of Business Depressions*, New York: Northeastern Press, 1922, Frank Tenney, *The American Journal of Philology* Vol. 56, No. 4 (1935), pp. 336–341, M. K. Thornton and R. L. Thornton, The Financial Crisis of A.D. 33: A Keynesian Depression? *The Journal of Economic History*, Vol. 50, No. 3 (Sep., 1990), pp. 655–662 and Cosmo Rodewald, *Money in the Age of Tiberius*, Tolowa, NJ: Rowman and Littlefield, 1976, pp. 1–17. For the original source, see Tacitus (*Ann*. VI, 16–17)

The information on Joseph Meged was taken from contemporary issues of *The New York Times*. A review of Roosevelt's implementation of the New Deal can be found in Arthur M. Schlesinger, Jr., *The Coming of the New Deal, 1933–1935, (The Age of Roosevelt, Vol. 2)*, Boston: Houghton Mifflin, 2003. For a book critical of the NRA and Roosevelt's economic policies, see Burton W. Folsom Jr., *New Deal or Raw Deal*, New York: Threshold Editions, 2009.

The equity risk premium was first discussed in detail in Rajnish Mehra and Edward C. Prescott, "The Equity Premium: A Puzzle," *Journal of Monetary Economics*, 15 (2) (1985), 145–161 and as a follow up, Rajnish Mehra and Edward C. Prescott, "The Equity Premium Puzzle in Retrospect," In G.M. Constantinides, M. Harris and R. Stulz. *Handbook of the Economics of Finance*. Amsterdam: North Holland. pp. 889–938, and Rajnish Mehra, *Handbook of the Equity Risk Premium*, Boston: Elsevier Science, 2007. Elroy Dimson, Paul Marsh and Mike Staunton, *Triumph of the Optimists, 101 Years of Global Investment Returns*, Princeton: Princeton University Press, 2002 provides a multi-country analysis of the equity risk premium.

Dr. Bryan Taylor is President and Chief Economist for Global Financial Data. He received his Ph.D. from Claremont Graduate University in Economics writing about the economics of the arts. He has taught both economics and finance at numerous universities in southern California and in Switzerland. He began putting together the Global Financial Database in 1990, collecting and transcribing financial and economic data from historical archives around the world. Dr. Taylor has published numerous articles and blogs based upon the Global Financial Database, the US Stocks Database, the UK Stocks Database and the GFD Indices, all collected by Global Financial Data over the past 25 years. Dr. Taylor's research has uncovered previously unknown aspects of financial history. He has written two books on financial history, a novel and several short stories. He resides in a Southern California Beach community with his dogs, Trouble and Shadow.

9 780999 548837